William Walsh

V. S. Naipaul

Oliver & Boyd
Edinburgh

Oliver & Boyd

Croythorn House,
23 Ravelston Terrace,
Edinburgh, EH4 3TJ
(A division of Longman Group Limited.)

© Text William Walsh 1973

0 05 0025880 Hardback
0 05 0025872 Paperback

Printed in Great Britain by
Cox & Wyman Ltd, London, Fakenham and Reading

The 'Modern Writers' series

The following titles in this new series of short guides to contemporary international writers will be available shortly:—

In Press

SOLZHENITSYN   Christopher Moody
SYLVIA PLATH   Eileen Aird
GUENTER GRASS   Irene Leonard
PHILIP LARKIN   David Timms

In Preparation

BORGES   J. M. Cohen
ROBERT LOWELL   J. F. Crick

Contents

Acknowledgments

For permission to quote from the works of V. S. Naipaul acknowledgments are due to André Deutsch Limited. The publishers also wish to make due acknowledgment to the following: Francis Wyndham, *The London Magazine* and *The Listener* for the extracts reprinted from two articles by him appearing in these journals; V. S. Naipaul, Jim Douglas Henry and *The Listener* for quotations from 'An Interview with V. S. Naipaul'; Faber and Faber Ltd. for material reprinted from *The West Indian Novel and its Background* by Kenneth Ramchand; and Oxford University Press for permission to reprint extracts from 'The Ironic Approach' by Gordon Rohlehr, included in *The Islands in Between: Essays on West Indian Literature*, edited with an introduction by Louis James (1968).

1   Early Work

Vidiadhar Surajprasad Naipaul was born in 1932 to a Hindu family in Trinidad. His grandfather, an indentured worker, was from Uttar Pradesh. The family were Brahmins, the modes and forms of life at home profoundly Indian, and Naipaul has retained to this day characteristic Brahmin delicacies and repugnancies: 'It still horrifies me that people should put out food for animals on plates that they themselves use; as it horrified me at school to see boys sharing Popsicles and Palates, local iced lollies; as it horrifies me to see women sipping from ladles with which they stir their pots.'[1] But although the family abounded in pundits he was an unbeliever, who took no pleasure in religious ceremonies and did not even understand the language. He was an agnostic almost as a child in a devout, orthodox family. There was, then, a break in the continuity between Naipaul and family life; there was also a break between the tone and quality of this family life and life in the general society outside. Within, there was the absolute certainty of the Indian inheritance, an unfractured psychic tranquillity, even when this was unaccompanied by any conscious acceptance of its religious and metaphysical premises; outside, the agitated life of modern Trinidad which turned out to be 'the extreme susceptibility of people who are unsure of themselves and, having no taste or style of their own, are eager for instruction'.[2] Naipaul himself was never at home or happy in Trinidad. 'When I was in the fourth form I wrote a vow on the endpaper of my *Kennedy's Revised Latin Primer* to leave within five years. I left after six; and for many years afterwards in England, falling asleep in bedsitters with the electric fire on, I had been awakened by the nightmare that I was back in tropical Trinidad.'[3]

Trinidad as Naipaul experienced it, was a discouraging context for a boy conscious of capacity if unsure how to realise it. The only professions were those of law and medicine, the successful commission agents, bank managers, members of the distributive trades: 'It was a place where the stories were never stories of success but of failure: brilliant men, scholarship winners, who had died young, gone mad, or taken to drink . . .'[4] Skill was taken to be conceit and it had to be cut down—or as the Trinidadians said, 'boiled down'. Naipaul, who was educated at the great school in Trinidad, Queen's Royal College, and then at University College, Oxford, tried hard to find a place in society after he came down from University. But it was impossible and he has lived and worked in England for many years now. He had no belief in his family religion or its way of life, which were in any case losing spring and power. The juxtaposed world of Trinidad offered no setting for his talent and no opportunity for its development. On the one side 'a peasant-minded, money-minded community, spiritually static because cut off from its roots, its religion reduced to rites without philosophy, set in a materialist colonial society . . .';[5] on the other, the community of the West Indian Negro lacerated by his desire to define his position in the world, and increasingly at odds, for both historical and economic reasons, with his Indian brother. Indeed, the race problem in Trinidad is not the opposition of black and white but the tension between Negro and Indian.

Naipaul's first novel, *The Mystic Masseur*, was published in 1957, *The Suffrage of Elvira* in 1958, *Miguel Street* in 1959. Since then he has produced four other novels, *A House for Mr. Biswas* (1961), *Mr. Stone and the Knights Companion* (1963), *The Mimic Men* (1967), and in 1971 his latest work *In A Free State*; a collection of short stories, *A Flag on the Island* (1967), a history of Trinidad, *The Loss of El Dorado* (1969), and two volumes of—what are they?—travel, analysis, documentation, perhaps autobiography, one on the West Indies, *The Middle Passage* (1962), the other on India, *An Area of Darkness* (1964). He has collected a whole sheaf of literary prizes, the Hawthornden Prize, the Somerset Maugham Award, The Llewellyn Rhys Memorial Prize, the Phoenix Trust Award and, this year, the Booker Prize for *In A Free State*. His readers, therefore, both private and official, have not been unappreciative, nor has his publisher, since he has honoured him at an early age with a collected edition, a prize usually awarded to the illustrious dead. So much esteem might well have sunk, or at least spoiled, a lesser talent. It has had no such effect on Naipaul, who is undoubtedly a writer of the utmost devotion, as well as a man of rare personal integrity.

Writing does not come easy to Naipaul, according to himself. He doesn't see himself as a born writer, although he used as a boy to watch his father trying to write stories. One has to have luck to enable the miracle to occur and an idea to give it the chance of happening: '. . . the act of writing, or devising a story or form, is such an artificial thing; you have to woo life into this artificial thing . . .'[6] One feels true creative effort in the necessity Naipaul feels to expel everything extraneous from himself in order to conceive the idea of a novel, in order to register the experience, in order at once to let it occur and realise it in words and fiction. And yet the thing about Naipaul is that he does seem above all other things, *a natural writer*; as I wrote elsewhere,[7] 'He is not simply *a* but *the* writer, all his private nature absorbed in his function as artist. He is not only a natural writer but a natural novelist. Themes for him assume the forms of action and ideas appeal to him only in so far as they satisfy, for him as for Henry James, "the appetite for the illustrational". He never, as some West Indian writers do, gives the impression that he is writing from the will, or that he is preaching a party line or some ethical imperative. His vision is his own, unenervated by contemporary social clichés or political routines. He is independent but also relevant. He is engaged with the stresses and strains we recognise as crucial in our experience now. His writing is nervous and present. This, together with the mixture in him of creeds, cultures and continents, with his expatriate career, his being able to practise an art in and of totally dissimilar worlds, all gives him a peculiarly contemporary quality.'

It is the life of Trinidad, its workers, peasants, crooks, shop-keepers, local politicians, pundits, which is treated in Naipaul's early novels, *The Mystic Masseur*, *The Suffrage of Elvira*, and *Miguel Street*, treated with gaiety, malice, the clearest insight, and with an unfailingly lucid and elegant line. It is the world described discursively, and sometimes bitterly, in *A Middle Passage*, a place where neither civilisation nor revolution had been created, only plantations and prosperity, neglect and decline. It was a country of peasants and shanty towns, '. . . the wooden houses, jalousied

3

half-way down, with fretwork along gables and eaves, fashionable before the concrete era; the concrete houses with L-shaped verandas and projecting front bedrooms, fashionable in the thirties; the two-storeyed Syrian houses in patterned concrete blocks, the top floor repeating the lower, fashionable in the forties.'[8] It was an energetic, anarchic, cynical, dusty place: 'There were no local standards. In the refinements of behaviour, as in architecture, everything was left to the caprices of the individual. In the immigrant society, memories growing dim, there was no guiding taste. As you rose you evolved your own standards, and they were usually those of modernity. There was no guiding taste because there was no taste. In Trinidad education was not one of the things money could buy; it was something money freed you from. Education was strictly for the poor.'[9] The West Indian lived in a borrowed culture. He struggled constantly after the hollowed-out substance of white civilisation. He needed, more than others, 'writers to tell him who he is and where he stands.'[10] But he expected his novels, like his advertisements, to have a detergent purpose. The Trinidadian was a society torn by the Negro's necessity to assert himself and the Indian's contempt for the Negro, so that the two races were more apart than when Froude noticed their separation in 1887. There are two contrasts in this early work: one between the huddled disorder of the place, and the unqualified sharpness and clarity of the writer's definition. The barely controlled chaos, both of place and sensibility, is outlined with a controlled and absolute clarity. It is as though the defining form is not just an instrument of the writer's perception, but a protest of the wholeness of his self against the neurotic muddle of the surroundings. The other contrast is between the flatness and dreariness of village and town, graceless, mean, wretchedly thin, like the village of Fuente Grove: the contrast between this and the brilliance and liveliness of the people, a folk with a genius for vivacity, expressed in an idiom of dancing vitality and wit.

The idiom is the one triumphant creation of the people, an expression of its whole nature, and it is the one mode of speech in which all are at home and accessible to one another, even those like Ganesh in *The Mystic Masseur* who are capable of using 'correct' English. It is sly, allusive, densely physical, threaded with disillusion, exquisitely comic. It is starred with proper names which carry the intonation of a society in which everything is familiar, every figure placed, every attachment recognised and judged; it is crammed with adjectives used as verbs, suggesting how a state, a feeling, becomes an activity with a beginning and an end; at the same time it abounds with impersonal terms of speech, and expressions with neutral subjects, even when they have to deal with persons, a habit which hints at what appears to be the condition of men, namely that for all their action and decision and deviousness, they are the victims of fundamentally incomprehensible and frequently malevolent forces. The intimate, energetic, sometimes brutal, speech of the people, contrasts with the lucidity and the silken run of the author's own voice, which has a near-Latin order and assurance, and which speaks out of a more inclusive intelligence and for a scheme of values in which judgment is an essential part of registration, and a detached and cultivated irony a key element in the sensibility.

The collocation of the two kinds of discourse, one thick and close to the ground, the other more finished and distant, especially when each is adjusted to the other with Naipaul's fineness of accommodation and tact, contributes markedly to the full and orchestrated effect given even by the earliest writing, even by the first novel, *The Mystic Masseur*. It is an effect calling both on the range of difference in human speech and the manifold capacities of the author. *The Mystic Masseur* rehearses the career or transformation of the ungainly Ganesh into the guru, of the failed primary school teacher and clumsy masseur into the healing mystic. Poor Ganesh had very little on his side; he was neither appealing nor well-placed. If not dim he was not really bright, and never succeeded in becoming more than a mediocre student at Queen's Royal College, where his father had scraped the money to send him before his untimely death. He even looked absurd. He had started school dressed in a khaki suit and a khaki topee. He never got over his country belief that reading except in daylight was damaging to the eyes; 'he went to sleep with the hens and woke before the cocks'. What was in his favour was a strange and apparently unfounded belief, dim at first, but no matter how frequent his failures, hardening into conviction, a belief in his own genius, the form or purpose of which he could not grasp, but the reality of which he accepted with complete certainty. He carried his gift before him cupped in his hands, invisible to himself as well as to others, but undoubtedly there. (Naturally he believed strongly in predestination: he had no other evidence for his distinction.) He had from the beginning a strong feeling of being separate from the villagers among whom he lived in Fuente Grove. Perhaps this was a function of an Indian talent for detachment, and perhaps in a West Indian society of almost hectic intimacy this worked to enforce his impressive quality.

Indian stability, West Indian mobility: not an inaccurate description of the feel of this novel. It needed the special condition of change in West Indian society at this moment, the gap between the outgoing administration and the establishment of an indigenous one on a solid basis, to make it possible for a part-eccentric, part-swindler like Ganesh to come to political prominence. But this is a most aromatically Indian work, the cuisine rice, dahl and sweet pink drinks; the costume dhoti, koortah and turban; the decorations in Ganesh's house, when he had become a well-paid mystic, the bright clashing colours of India and two stone elephants, designed by himself. His first work was a brochure called *101 questions and answers on the Hindu Religion*. The Caribbean made it possible for Ganesh to emerge from rural obscurity, but the characters in the novel are almost exclusively Indian. Indeed, the only two non-Indians are an old African flirting with Hinduism who then elects for Mohammedanism, warning the Hindus incidentally what they may then expect from him, and a slightly touched Englishman, also flirting with Hinduism, who dresses in the saffron of a holy man and suffers the scolding of the little boys. The core of the fiction, the change which is both magical and inevitable, from con-man into man worthy of confidence, is an ancient theme in Indian writing, and it has been treated by another distinguished novelist, in a purely Indian setting, by R. K. Narayan in *The Guide*. He ends, it is true, with Raju the protagonist as a martyr, whereas Ganesh concludes as a politician. There is a difference, too, in the treatment. Narayan's is light and tolerant, Naipaul's mischievous and sceptical. But there is a deeper resemblance. Narayan's Raju responds to a want in the nature of the peasants around him, and it is the vacancy in West Indian society, the lack of a hero or centre or focus, which makes possible the farcical career of Ganesh, who blends cunning, stupidity, ignorance and will-power, into an extraordinary recipe for success.

Naipaul's prose style lacks any awkwardness or arbitrary flush; it is wholly free of the gratuitous and the gesturing. Indeed, it may well seem mild and unemphatic. But it is also lithe, sharp and definitive. Its grace is no block to a questing analytic capacity. It corresponds in its quiet firmness to some central assurance in the author, and it is this medium which makes it possible for him to fit together, in the way I noted above, a variety of idiom and conversational habits. It corresponds, too, to an unbending honesty, the moral equivalent of clarity of perception, and it is a power which enables Naipaul to see not only Ganesh but minor characters in all their contradictory complexity and depth. He is a master of tone, with a capacity to differentiate one from another and the further power to assemble a variety of tones in consort. The slummocky and sweating Ramlogan, the rumshop keeper, and his near-Dickensian daughter, Leela, who becomes Ganesh's wife (this is how it appears to happen: she is more wished on Ganesh than wished for), the devoted friend, the nervous, nibbling Beharry, the splendid managing woman called The Great Belcher, these and others, each precisely differentiated, and each calling upon and exposing a different element in Ganesh's nature, together make, for all that there are no more than a dozen or so, a world packed with contrast but single in its inward likeness. Each of the minor characters, one feels, is experienced as more than a mere surface or dimension, and yet each is transparent, totally seen and communicated. Ganesh, on the other hand, has at the heart of his nature an impervious core, something one cannot grasp or mould, and something we realise that he himself cannot comprehend or manage. Each part of the design supports and realises more fully the strange, comic, faintly sinister, ulti-mately valid and self-authenticating personality of the mystic masseur.

Naipaul's comedy is not one of situation or plot; nor are the characters cartoons or puppets; and if it is satirical that is only so because of the author's sense of the ridiculous and his eye for dishonesty. It has been called malicious but it is hard to see why,

7

since the attitude is neither contemptuous nor patronising—if they are different—and the author can hardly be condemned for not having as his purpose the wrapping up of reality in cosy illusion. It is a comedy essentially of the individual person in his damaged society, the actual person and the observed setting. It is always open to such comedy, and particularly when written by a writer with a gift for modulating one tone into another without dissonance or distraction, to strike a serious note. Even the gayest, the most deliriously comic persons, are frayed with anxieties and hunted by sickness and death. Here is a passage, for example, from quite early on in *The Mystic Masseur*, when Ganesh is hauled out of school to attend his father's burial service;[11]

> 'Don't come with me,' Ganesh said. 'I want to be alone'.
> He didn't know what he thought or felt but he didn't
> want to cry and left the room. They were waiting for
> him to come out and quickly encircled him. He heard
> Ramlogan saying, 'Come on, man, give the boy air.
> Is his father dead, you know. His only father.' And the
> wailing began again. . . .
> He remembered applying the last caste-marks to the
> old man's forehead, and doing many more things until
> it seemed that ritual had replaced grief.

This passage and its context shows the characteristically cool manner, the eye unblurred by any subjectivity, the detail establishing a world which is solidly *there*, and the totally illustrated meaning. It shows the boy's senses heightened by tension, and makes us hear the 'sobs and shrieks and lamentations' which suggest both a genuine grief and an enjoyable social duty. And it concludes with a generalisation or reflection which wells up naturally from its source in the situation. We realise that not only Ganesh, but all the members of the community, are working to replace grief with ritual, that this is indeed the mark not only of their lives, difficult and constricted as they are, but of life itself.

But of course one could modify Naipaul's phrase and speak not of a grief, but an experience replacing a ritual. Democracy in action, as interpreted by the villagers in *The Suffrage of Elvira*, turns the incomprehensible and ancient ritual of election, meaningless as it is and without any sanction in their own history, into a complicated if miniature ballet of power-politics—which is itself an extension of the war waged within the family, and a genuine experience for them therefore. 'Democracy had come to Elvira four years before, in 1946; but it had taken nearly everybody by surprise and it wasn't until 1950, a few months before the second general election under universal adult franchise, that people began to see the possibilities.' The possibilities are as remarkable, as weird, and as fundamentally human, as the observance of religion in the same village:[12]

> Things were crazily mixed up in Elvira. Everybody, Hindus, Muslims and Christians, owned a Bible; the Hindus and Muslims looking on it, if anything, with greater awe. Hindus and Muslims celebrated Christmas and Easter. The Spaniards and some of the negroes celebrated the Hindu festival of lights.

The possibilities that people of this degree of caution and comprehensiveness could see in an election are indeed remarkable. Religion, rum, family jealousies, obeah, the care of the sick and the spotting of the moribund, together with a generous sprinkling of more modern devices, loudspeaker vans, car cavalcades, the sugar of dollars, when brewed together transform the bleakness of democracy into 'the election bacchanal'.

'In God we trust, as the saying goes . . . In man we bust. *As* the saying goes': this apophthegm of Ramlogan engagingly insinuates the Trinidadian scepticism about the goodness of man, although with people so resilient and infinitely pliant as the inhabitants of Elvira, one doubts that it will be man who will bust. The characters are marked throughout by an indelible and powerful individuality, even the dimmest of them. Certainly one could not conceive of any of the protagonists in this election campaign, conducted like a chess game in which the rules and the players change with every move, 'busting', when they include the despairing but confident candidate Surujpat ('Pat') Harbans, the miniature, menacing insect of a man Chittaranjan the goldsmith, the rum-soaked Baksh and his enormous, prolific wife ('Everybody just washing their foot and jumping in this democracy business.

9

But I promising you, for all the sweet it begin sweet, it going to end damn sour'), the opposing campaign manager Baksh's sunglassed son, Foam, his rival Lorkhoor ('This is the voice of the ever-popular Lorkhoor . . . begging you and imploring you and entreating you and beseeching you . . .'). The manœuvring is Machiavellian in its delicacy and ferocity, the language of the hustings crackling with insult and innuendo and laced with a heady rum of proverbs.

But the extravagance of personality, matched by the wildness of the action, mixing as it does blackmail, magic, persuasion, calculation and accommodation, never degenerates into romp or farce. There is always present the control of the fastidious mind of a conscious artist. One is also aware under the surface of the zany behaviour, of hints of other kinds of experience, of real human anger or disaster, of the venom of village life and the sudden shock of real feeling, as when the virtue of Chittaranjan's daughter is questioned by a frantic neighbour, and one suddenly feels the cold, radical tremor of the horrified Hindu soul.

The Mystic Masseur is organised around a person, *The Suffrage of Elvira* around an event, and the third of this triad of early works, *Miguel Street*, around a place. The characters who loll and saunter through the streets have the same glittering oddity, but the intimations of grimness, latent in the two earlier books, assume a harder, more insistent form in *Miguel Street*. The book is composed of a set of more than a dozen sketches of the street's inhabitants, from the tough Bogart who turns out to be a not very successful bigamist, to Pope the carpenter, who works constantly making 'the thing without a name', to Eddoes, the lean driver of the blue cart, the municipal disposal unit, to Mr. Titus Hoyt, I.A. (London, external), the teacher, and B. Wordsworth, the uncreative and finally despairing poet. They are unified not just by the sensibility of the place but by the consciousness of the young boy who observes them. His alert, calm scrutiny, uncomprehending of certain adult nuances but in other ways more penetrating than any adult's, is beautifully and obliquely established. There is not even a touch of sentimental softness in this delicately fixed portrait of the child, although there is, I think, in the one failure of the book, the sketch of B. Wordsworth, a faintly gluey effect, possibly the result of Naipaul the writer's sympathy for the plight of another, suffering, literary man. The peculiar savour of the book comes from the application of a severe and sophisticated intelligence to conduct of the utmost naïvety, and from the further paradox that the crazily ingenuous activity of the people—one realises it gradually—is bedded in a set of inarticulate but profound convictions about the nature of human existence, the burden of which is the classical and stoic view caught in the comment by Hat on the death of Lorna, the young girl who brought her baby home to a house already swarming with the product of her philoprogenitive mama: 'Life is helluva thing. You can see trouble coming and you can't do a damn thing to prevent it coming. You just got to sit and watch and wait.'

Life in Miguel Street is lived, at least by the men, outside, on the pavement. The women, the power centre of the family, live a less external existence out of a caustic sense of disillusioned reality. 'You know, Mrs. Hereira,' says the mother of the 'I' of the stories, to a romantic white woman who has deserted her husband for the brutish and drunken Tony, 'You know, Mrs. Hereira, I really wish you was like me. If somebody did marry you off when you was fifteen, we wouldnta been hearing all this nonsense, you hear. Making all this damn fuss about your heart and love and all that rubbish.' Love in this sense, as distinct from sex, doesn't occupy too much of the consciousness of those beating out a living in Miguel Street. They are too much aware of the helplessness of the subject, too obviously witnesses to the brutality of events. What they look for in conduct is not conformity to blander values, but that it be stamped with the seal of the authentic self. If it is, even brutality, even the beating of wives and children, is tolerable. Affectation, hypocrisy, self-deception, these are the condemned qualities. These people, so brilliantly themselves, have a strangely avian and mobile habit of life. A flash and they are gone, another and they are back. Everyone accepts these unaccountable disappearances as a natural part of the treacherous instability of events, and perhaps as a condition of surviving their implacable advance. One has to develop on this street a style of self and a style of living, and human morality is essentially a matter in which action follows the correct logic of character. At the same time, man's helplessness in the face of life is reflected in the limitations of intelligence in understanding it. Not only in events, not only in circumstances, but in people themselves, both to themselves and as they are seen by others, there are pockets of incomprehensible, inexplicable darkness. A man is a set of activities fastened around an enigmatic knot, like Popo making 'the thing without a name', or Man Man who never worked, but was never idle. 'He was hypnotised by the word, particularly the written word, and he would spend a whole day writing a single word.' The others are not hypnotised by the word, but entranced with it, and they use it with a poetic, vigorous power which suggests something both of the painful complexity of their lives, and the energy with which they manage them. What disillusion, sharpness and experience are gathered up in the reply of the boy's mother to the neighbour about her son's scholarship 'to study drugs' in England, this being the only scholarship available:

> The news got to Elias and he took it badly. He came to the gate one evening and shouted, 'Bribe, bribe. Is all you could do. Bribe.'
> My mother shouted back, 'The only people who does complain about bribe is those who too damn poor to have anything to bribe with.'

I used at one time to take a somewhat narrower, less positive view of these early novels, both as to their intrinsic merit and their place in the author's development. For example, in 1970 I wrote:[13]

> The combination of peasant sagacity and cultivated intelligence, of muscle and nerve, in *Miguel Street*, *The Mystic Masseur* and *The Suffrage of Elvira* makes the books which are fed from regional springs and realised in regional detail more than simply regional. There are murmurations in them all of a more inclusive humanity. And yet, and yet . . . These novels communicate an air of capability, of sinewy resource, which seems more extensive than the matter being dealt with. Their richness, after all, resides in minute perfections and their force is a limited and contained one. The reader is aware of considerable powers put to rather too markedly

a parochial purpose. There is perhaps a shade too
much emphasis on charm. One begins to long for
something more severe and more testing. One wants to
feel not just powers in the author but power in the
work. . . . If one wanted to specify one's uneasiness
about the first three novels it would have to do, I
think, with one's sense of a certain discrepancy between
the perfection of the surface and the inclusiveness of
the theme. The surface connects, it seems, only with a
vague depth whereas one feels it requires to be supported
with something more powerful and profound: 'requires',
that is, if the significance of the work is to be level
with the capacity of the author.

This judgment is fair enough as it stands. It is, however, clearly
grounded on the achievement of Naipaul's masterpiece, *A House
for Mr. Biswas*, and it is somewhat deficient in historical sympathy,
taking as it does so little account of the place of these three early
novels in the development of the author's powers. Without this
preliminary work he could hardly have matured to the point at
which he was ready for the major undertaking of *A House for
Mr. Biswas*. Moreover, the judgment hardly stresses sufficiently
the existence in these early books, particularly in *Miguel Street*,
of what I called 'intimations of grimness', those notes towards a
more tragic view of life, which arrive at their full existence in
Mr. Biswas.

In any case, the limitation suggested in my judgment is quite
different in tone from the somewhat patronising response these
early novels had from English reviewers on their appearance, and
from the hostility of reaction they provoked in the West Indies,
particularly among some of their most distinguished writers. This
point has been dealt with with the necessary firmness and discrimination by Francis Wyndham in an admirable critique:[14]

During the fifties it was considered rather bad form, in
literary circles, to approach an 'underdeveloped country'
in a spirit of sophisticated humour; and it was
therefore perhaps unfortunate for V. S. Naipaul that
his first three books happened to be social comedies set

in Trinidad. Well-meaning British reviewers—whether in sheer ignorance of the background, or else unconsciously reflecting the prevalent attitudes of neo-colonialist embarrassment—responded to *The Mystic Masseur*, *The Suffrage of Elvira* and *Miguel Street* in dismayed tones of patronising rebuke. They would have preferred a simple study in compassion where a clear distinction is made between the oppressors and the oppressed, or a 'charming' exercise in the *faux-naif*, or a steamily incoherent drama of miscegenation and primitive brutality. The West Indian public, with a refinement of irony, expressed a similar reaction—thus proving that the recent confusions of neo-colonialist liberalism had already travelled as far as the original imperialist settlers and taken roots as deep. In 1958 the *Times Literary Supplement* published an article by Naipaul in which he mischievously transposed some of the sillier remarks made about his early novels in order to reveal the gratuitous insult hidden within them: 'Imagine a critic in Trinidad writing of *Vile Bodies*: "Mr. Evelyn Waugh's whole purpose is to show how funny English people are. He looks down his nose at the land of his birth. We hope that in future he writes of his native land with warm affection."'

2   Travel, Documentation, History

Naipaul, I have said, is a natural novelist. His themes, his thought, are sunk deep in his fiction; his ideas are the distillation of the particular experience he is engaged with in the given novel. His is a concrete not an abstract intelligence. But this doesn't mean that it is not an intelligence of a formidable and impressive kind, because it certainly is. It is nimble, sharp, neither easily put off by the routine explanation nor enveloped in any modern haze. His mind is not weighed down by any heavy inherited Indian burden, biased by subjective and arbitrary convictions, or hag-ridden by self-pity. His is a very clear and naked intelligence: his only prejudice is to be in favour of reality. This respect for, this fidelity to, what is the case, has as its instrument an eye of a very fine and discriminating sort, and a corresponding skill in notation. That air of detachment which many have noted in Naipaul, and which sometimes may seem, and indeed be, evidence of an intention to keep his distance from the world, is more frequently, and certainly at its best, a discipline of scrupulous accuracy, the effort to define the fact and refine the feeling. *Spectator ab extra*: Coleridge's words about Wordsworth, are peculiarly appropriate to the nature of Naipaul's sensibility. He has the telescopic sight of the unattached observer, who is not only a creative observer, even an observer of genius, but one in whom observation feeds reflection, and one in whom the observation of others leads to analysis of self.

It is natural, then, that Naipaul's two books of travel, *The Middle Passage* (1962), a return to the Caribbean, and *An Area of Darkness* (1964), a journey through India, brilliant in their evo-cation of place and quick with lucid, questing intelligence, should become explorations of self. In the first he examines his immediate antecedents, the physical and social conditions of his childhood in the West Indies, in the second the remoter geography and history

of his Indian forbears in India itself. In both he is moving, sometimes crawling painfully, up through the obscure, bending tunnels
of the self. He has a vivid awareness of place as a part of experience, and experience as both an influence upon but also an
extension of the constitution of the self. So that while the tone is
cool and the description of landscape, feeling, background and
ground underfoot never fudged or romanticised, one is conscious
that he is treating not just external objects, but grappling, in-
directly, it may be, as with a lock fastened upon one part of the
wrestler's body which is meant to affect another, grappling with
the mysteries of personal awareness and being. There are dangers
for a novelist in such an undertaking, consequences, as Leavis
puts it: 'of queering one discipline with the habits of another.'[1]

More obvious dangers perhaps lay in the circumstances of the
journey back to the West Indies. Its occasion was a travelling
scholarship granted by the government of Trinidad and Tobago
and a suggestion by the Premier that Naipaul should write a book
about the West Indies. Dr. Williams, himself a scholar, showed a
restraint unusual among politicians and neither he nor his
government made any effort to influence Naipaul, whose integrity,
as unsparing to himself as to others, was not in any case open to
this kind of temptation. The real danger was more of the kind
hinted at by Leavis. Could not a novelist whose habit is above all
to illustrate, to embody, easily have this precious faculty damaged
by the necessity for a discursive and analytic method? 'The novelist works towards conclusions of which he is often unaware; and
it is better that he should. To analyse and decide before writing
would rob the writer of the excitement which supports him during
his solitude, and would be the opposite of my method as a novelist.
I also felt it as a danger that, having factually analysed the
society as far as I was able, I would be unable afterwards to
think of it in terms of fiction and that in anything I might write
I would be concerned only to prove a point.'[2]

The uncharacteristically graceless phrases, '. . . having factually
analysed the society . . .' and '. . . to think of it in terms of
fiction . . .', suggest, perhaps, a certain chapping of the artist's
conscience at having even to face such problems. But that the
danger was one he learned to glide by in a smooth, untroubled way,
is certainly confirmed by the quality of the later work. His suc-

cess indeed in these two travel books comes from not allowing the discursive method completely to oust the novelist's habit. There is no generalisation which is not firmly tethered in detail, no reflection which is not grounded in the reaction to a specific experience. The analysis is supported throughout by the novelist's skill in shaping a subject, in establishing a figure, implying a background, hinting at a theme. The level of explicitness of generalisation and analysis never becomes purely abstract. It is constantly qualified by the intrusion of awkward reality, insistently weighed down by the palpable, by experience seen, felt, smelt, heard.

In *The Middle Passage* the key figure is Naipaul himself, tranquil within, tense in his relationships; the subject is the social and physical character of the several West Indian territories; the background is the West Indies of Naipaul's childhood, looming through, or immanent in the firmly summoned contemporary Caribbean presence; the theme is his childhood fear of Trinidad. The densely realised actuality of the West Indies gradually reveals the influences that went to form the sensibility of Naipaul, so that the work is not only a diary of travel but the journal of an identity. And since Naipaul is a highly cultivated man with a taste for scholarship and considerable historical knowledge, the day-to-day events of his passage are accompanied by voices from the past. Indeed, travel, as he understands it, is the documentation of history.

His treatment of the journey brings out the manifold variety of West Indian societies. Each has its own specific individuality according to which of the many national influences came to grip at that point, the Spanish, the British, the French, the Dutch, the African, the Indian, and the Amerindian. Martinique is impregnated with France's *mission civilisatrice*, although the prejudices of the French bourgeoisie have coalesced with racial distinctions derived from slavery to produce the most racially discriminating society in the West Indies. It is a place where 'dinner table gossip is the most sanctimonious and the most assassinating I have ever heard'. In Surinam the Dutch have been able to generate a genuine affection for Holland, and there are no acute racial problems. Nevertheless, it is racked with an ex-colonial nationalism in which 'the Negro in particular is bewildered and irritable'. In the mainland territory of British Guiana, where 600,000 people live in a country the size of Britain, a fertile, empty land is torn by the antipathy of African and Indian. It is hard in Trinidad to find reminders of slavery since the Spanish slave code was surprisingly the least inhumane of all, and it was easier under that code than any other for a slave to buy his freedom. While it is hard in Trinidad to find reminders of slavery, they cannot be avoided in the rest of the West Indies, and certainly not in Jamaica, where the peasants, speaking the purest English of all West Indians, live in the same world but at a carefully preserved distance from the deracinated luxury of the northern resorts— 'turquoise sea, white sands, reverential bowtie, black servants, sunglassed figures below striped umbrellas', and both coexist with the huddles of board and cardboard and canvas and tin choked together on damp rubbish dumps, which are the slums of Kingston.

The nationalism of Surinam is a movement of intellectuals rejecting the culture of Europe; Ras Tafarianism in Jamaica is nothing more than a proletarian extension of this attitude, carried to its crazy and logical limit. In Trinidad nationalism is an impossibility since every man has to exist for himself and to grasp whatever dignity and power he can. 'He owed no loyalty to the island and scarcely any to his group.' Trinidad is a country in which there is no set way of doing anything: 'every house can be a folly. There is no set way of dressing or cooking or entertaining. Everyone can live with whoever he can get wherever he can afford. Ostracism is meaningless.' Trinidad is the land of the complete anarchist and the natural eccentric. If the Trinidadian is without standards, he is also without sanctimoniousness, and never makes pleas for intolerance in the name of piety. 'Everything that makes the Trinidadian an unreliable, exploitable citizen makes him a quick, civilized person whose values are always human ones, whose standards are only those of wit and style.'

Variety, oddity, the multiplication of human differences: this is the impression formed in the reader as he follows Naipaul's discovering, disconcerting journey. But he becomes aware also, through the oblique reminders of history and the voices of nineteenth-century travellers, of the fact of continuity. The flow of time keeps to certain channels. James Anthony Froude's *The English in the West Indies* (1887), for example, in spite of his knotty

Victorian bias and his unmitigated racial prejudice, is a work which constantly surprises by its current cogency. Here is a passage from Froude which Naipaul uses in his epigraph:

> They were valued only for the wealth which they yielded, and society there had never assumed any particularly noble aspect. There has been splendour and luxurious living, and there have been crimes and horrors, and revolts and massacres. There has been romance, but it has been the romance of pirates and outlaws. The natural graces of life do not show themselves under such conditions. There has been no saint in the West Indies since Las Casas, no hero unless philonegro enthusiasm can make one out of Toussaint. There are no people there in the true sense of the word, with a character and purpose of their own.

And here is Naipaul's version of this judgment in the modern world: 'Again and again one comes back to the main, degrading fact of the colonial society; it never required efficiency, it never required quality, and these things, because unrequired, became undesirable.'[3] Again, 'The two races [the Indian and Negro], Froude observed in 1887, are more absolutely apart than the white and the black, the Asiatic insists the more on his superiority in the fear perhaps that if he did not the white might forget it.'[4] And Naipaul: 'When people speak of the race problem in Trinidad they do not mean the Negro–white problem. They mean the Negro–Indian rivalry.'[5] 'He burns to be a scholar,' Trollope observed of the Negro, 'puzzles himself with fine words, addicts himself to religion for the sake of appearances, and delights in aping the little graces of civilisation. . . . "These people marry now"' [a white woman said to Trollope in Jamaica]. 'In the tone of her voice,' he comments, 'I thought I could catch an idea that she conceived them in doing so to be trenching on the privileges of their superiors.'[6] And Naipaul: 'This was the greatest damage done to the Negro by slavery. It taught him self-contempt. It set him the ideals of white civilization and made him despise every other. Deprived as a slave of Christianity, education and family, he set himself after emancipation to acquire these things;

and every step on the road to whiteness deepened the anomaly of his position and increased his vulnerability.'[7] The condition of continuity is true of smaller things. A hundred years ago Trollope complained about the state of the British Guiana coastal road—it was the only thing in British Guiana he disliked—and Naipaul reports that the road, made of burnt earth, hasn't improved since then. And not only the road, but the food. Trollope:

> But it is to be remarked all through the island that the people are fond of English dishes, and that they despise, or affect to despise, their own productions. They will give you ox-tail soup when turtle would be much cheaper. Roast beef and beefsteaks are found at almost every meal. An immense deal of beer is consumed. When yams, avocado pears, the mountain cabbage, plantains, and twenty other delicious vegetables may be had for the gathering, people will insist on eating bad English potatoes; and the desire for English pickles is quite a passion.[8]

And Naipaul: 'One of the complaints of tourists in Jamaica is that they cannot get Jamaican food. And once in a small intellectuals' club in Port of Spain I asked for guava jelly: they had only green-gage jam.'[9]

Travel reveals the fact of continuity not only in the history and character of the West Indian world, but in the traveller himself. When Naipaul lands in Trinidad from the *Francisco Bobadilla*, the years of his life and all his alien experience as expatriate and writer fall away. He does not arrive in the city as a stranger. He is not one of those who feel that special quality in the people of a city never seen before, that ... 'they are adepts in a ritual the traveller doesn't know... moving from one mystery to another'.[10] Naipaul is distressed not so much by familiarity as by the feeling of continuity. He is left not with any tingle at the novelty of a new town but with his ancient fear of Trinidad:

> I had never examined this fear of Trinidad. I had never wished to. In my novels I had only expressed this fear; and it is only now, at the moment of writing, that I am

> able to attempt to examine it. I knew Trinidad to be
> unimportant, uncreative, cynical. . . . Power was
> recognized, but dignity was allowed to no one. Every
> person of eminence was held to be crooked and
> contemptible. We lived in a society which denied
> itself heroes.[11]

It may be that that particular mark of the early novels, a quality of tightness and tautness, a suggestion that more is at hand than the gay material, comes from this disguised, controlled fear. The elegance and certainty are poised above some other seething force below. His travels in Trinidad so many years after the point of time when fear, or at least when fear as one of the expected tangle of motives, forced him into exile, enabled Naipaul to uncover the nightmare, to examine it with the novelist's objectivity and insight, and in doing so clearly to exorcise it. Now the vaguely terrifying shadows of childhood and the place which gave rise to them become Trinidad, 'a booming, vigorous, even frenzied little island', and Port of Spain, the noisiest city in the world, where one is stunned by the radios, the record players, the tape recorders, the steel bands.

What was once a hated landscape, flat, treeless and hot, organised about the sugar cane, that 'brutal plant, tall and grass-like, with rough, razor-edged blades', now becomes a plain, with 'walls of grass on either side . . . steel-blue plumes dancing above a grey-green carpet, grey-green because each long blade curves back on itself, revealing its paler underside'.[12] It is also now the country of inventive, imaginative speech; of cricket which has always been more than a game, the only activity which permitted a man to grow to his full stature and to be measured against international standards; the country, too, of the calypso, in which alone, according to Naipaul, the Trinidadian touches reality.

And finally, the West Indies reveals the tragic continuity of human action and human suffering. Perhaps the rest of the West Indies even more than Trinidad (but Trinidad too, in its own way), shows the tragic continuity of human history. The aftermath of history and the violence of race feeling are intimate and inescapable. When in his journey he saw race feeling he thought at first it was a purely local eruption, created by the pressures of local politics,

> But soon, on the journey I was now getting ready to
> make, I came to see that such eruptions were
> widespread, and represented feelings coming to the
> surface in Negro communities throughout the
> Caribbean; confused feelings, without direction; the
> Negro's rejection of the guilt he has borne for so long;
> the last, delayed Spartacan revolt, more radical than
> Toussaint l'Ouverture's; the closing of accounts this
> side of the middle passage.[13]

Naipaul's next journey, and further excavation of the self, was to territory even more inward than the West Indies, and to an area puzzlingly darker and further away than Trinidad. As the grandson of a labourer from the village of Dubes and Tiwaris, Brahmins of Utter Pradesh, India lay about him in his infancy; in the things of the house, the string bed, the coloured pictures of Hindu deities, the brass and sandalwood. It existed, too, in the secret premises of family action, in a profound ease of self-possession; but this unorthodox offspring of a highly orthodox family found the ritual absurd and distasteful and its traditional significance without meaning, in spite of any merits it had in style and continuity. So that when he came to India it was to see in sunlight the India that to the child had been overwhelmed in darkness. His journey to India had been slow, uncomfortable, but an appropriate preparation for the East:

> From Athens to Bombay another idea of man had defined
> itself by degrees, a new type of authority and subservience.[14]

When Naipaul arrived in India he brought with him a fastidious, independent personality, a considerable reputation as a novelist, and tastes and sensibilities not just well-bred but almost neurotically delicate, a result possibly of that Brahmin inheritance. He also brought with him an illusory intimacy, derived from his childhood, with the forms of Indian life and the modes of Indian feeling. It was illusory, at least, if it was expected to make for understanding, because the Indian ethos and Indian values, if they were internal to Naipaul's family, were external to Naipaul's spirit. The substance, above all the religion, which quickened them with life and endowed them with solidity and continuity, was incomprehensible and distasteful to Naipaul's intensely Western, almost protestant, intelligence which had long since opted for scepticism, openness, individuality, practicality, results.

The paradox of Naipaul's Indian journey was that he brought to bear upon the Indian scene a refinement of that superior, detached, Brahmin tradition drawn from India itself. This was joined with the barest acquaintance with India and even a superficial knowledge of Naipaul's work could have foretold the disaster of the impression India was to make on him. He is intent and focussed as a bird, as unsympathetic as a hawk and as high above the object. Naipaul's cool gaze sweeps over the subcontinent from Bombay to Kashmir, its capacity for observing unaffected both by his troubled soul or by the deadening poverty on every side.

What he is shaken by, what he returns to again and again, in an almost compulsive way, is the subject of defecation, the condition of public lavatories, the habits and oddities of Indians in these matters. One sometimes feels that to Naipaul India consists of nothing but people at stool. There is in Naipaul's attitude to dirt and squalor, as well as a general Western distaste for the crude ways of a desperately poor, fundamentally rural people, something of a Brahmin's horror for the unclean, and something too of Swift's mixture of microscopic attention and appalled recoil. It is in this strange context, in fact, that Naipaul speaks of Gandhi, emphasizing Gandhi's teaching on rural hygiene and the necessity for excreta to be buried in earth no deeper than nine to twelve inches, where the minute life, together with the light and air which easily penetrate, will turn the excreta into good, soft, sweet-smelling soil within the week. (This kind of information can be drawn from many places in the journal.) Gandhi looked at India as no Indian could, Naipaul claims, because he was in fact a colonial who settled finally in India only at the age of 46, with many years of experience of a wholly different country behind him. Here is a passage written out of that part of Naipaul's nature which is in sympathy with this, with *his*, version of Gandhi

23

and his doctrine. It is a description of four men washing down the steps of a seedy Bombay hotel. It shows Naipaul's care for exactness in defining atmosphere and action and his capacity to outline a scene so that it stands there, after a few spare strokes, solid and complete. At the same time we are also aware of the critical acumen which can offer the apt, lucid and explanatory generalisation. The enigmatic action becomes coherent. This is a comment that could fairly be offered at very many places in Naipaul's work. But in this particular passage there is in addition a strange quality of empathy. The sweepers are not just pointed at from outside but entered into. The empathy, however, is so strange because the immediacy of understood experience includes only feelings which are unloving and unforgiving; not those which usually inform the faculty of empathy. There is not a touch of pity for the humiliated men, only contempt for them and disgust with the system.

> Study these four men washing down the steps of this
> unpalatable Bombay hotel. The first pours water from a
> bucket, the second scratches the tiles with a twig broom,
> the third uses a rag to slop the dirty water down the
> steps into another bucket, which is held by the fourth.
> After they have passed, the steps are as dirty as before;
> but now above the blackened skirting-tiles the walls are
> freshly and dirtily splashed. The bathrooms and
> lavatories are foul; the slimy woodwork has rotted away
> as a result of this daily drenching; the concrete walls
> are green and black with slime. You cannot complain
> that the hotel is dirty. No Indian will agree with you.
> Four sweepers are in daily attendance, and it is enough
> in India that the sweepers attend. They are not required
> to *clean*. That is a subsidiary part of their function, which
> is to *be* sweepers, degraded beings, to go through the
> motions of degradation. They must stoop when they
> sweep; cleaning the floor of the smart Delhi café, they
> will squat and move like crabs between the feet of the
> customers, careful to touch no one, never looking up,
> never rising. In Jammu City you will see them
> collecting filth from the streets with their bare hands.

> This is the degradation the society requires of them,
> and to this they willingly submit. They are dirt; they
> wish to appear as dirt.[15]

Caste gaols a man in his private duties, while it serves to de-nude the function of its practical efficacy. So that in a system based on it action is volatilised into being and status frozen into state. In India, *esse sequitur operari*. According to Naipaul man *is* his proclaimed function. 'This is caste. In the beginning a no doubt useful division of labour in a rural society, it has now divorced function from social application, position from duty.' Action reduced to being weakens the importance of results and fortifies the instinct for symbolism. Gandhi himself in answer to this national bias became a Mahatma. 'The spinning wheel did not dignify labour, it was only absorbed into the great Indian symbolism.' The Mahatma has been absorbed into the formless spirituality and decayed pragmatism of India, parts of the eternal Indian effort to incorporate and nullify. 'The revolutionary became a god and his message was thereby lost.' He had become part of the ritual of symbolism which supports the Indian throughout life.

Enough has been said, mostly in Naipaul's own words, to indi-cate the anger and pain which this habitually calm observer, gazing at the vast Indian scene, finds in his response to it. It comes, I think, from a sense of violation and shock, and it tells us perhaps as much about Naipaul as about India. It is as much evidence about the subject as a report on the object. The fabled past, the myth, the rich and sacred sources of family certainties, are finally and devastatingly uncovered. The intensity of Naipaul's despair is related to the fact that in savaging India he is also savaging himself.

It is the Indian, the Brahmin, in Naipaul which accounts for the violence of his reaction to the soiled and impure. But Naipaul is also a remarkably free, untethered soul, an expatriate in his birthplace, an alien in his ancestral land, a disengaged observer of Britain and other countries. Mobility is the breath of life to him. It is not surprising, therefore, that he rejects with a kind of ferocity the sealed and stratified society of India. The force of degree in India, incorporating, locating, negating, is intolerable to him. No Indian could be an outsider, and to be able to act this part is essential to Naipaul, the temperamentally displaced person. The inner world which supports and nourishes the Indian system remains constant. 'Every man and woman is marked by destiny, on everyone fate has its eye . . . and so it happens that to one whole area of India a late seventeenth-century traveller like Ovington remains in many ways a valuable guide.'

Naipaul's journey, he conveys at the end of this book, was one that ought not to have been made. Racial similarity was no help to understanding. The people he met, rich and poor, remained incomprehensible to him, at once narrower and grander. 'Their choice in almost everything seemed more restricted than mine; yet they were clearly the inhabitants of a big country; they had an easy, unromantic comprehension of size. The landscape was hard and wrong. I could not relate it to myself. I was looking for the balanced rural landscape of Indian Trinidad.' He could not relate it to himself. The balance was wrong. *He* could not, and perhaps *it* was, because he was looking not at India but for some personal vision which India could not provide because it existed only within Naipaul. India could offer only a context for despair

Having purged his soul of India—the figure seems an appropriate one—Naipaul turns back to Trinidad, impelled by a necessity to resolve for himself the West Indian enigma at least. The remoter world of India stayed impervious, an area of darkness resistant to any explanatory light Naipaul was able to bring to it. Perhaps the more immediate riddle of Trinidad, enacted in his novels, discursively teased out in *The Middle Passage*, might yield at least a measure of its secrecy to an historical treatment. The examination of antecedents might reveal what scrutiny of the system could not. I should at once qualify the phrase, 'historical treatment'. Naipaul is fascinated with the past, but he is not a trained historian. The material of *The Loss of El Dorado* (1969) is historical, but the treatment is both imaginative and analytical, more a function of the exercise of the sensibility than of any strictly historical faculty.

The myth of El Dorado, the myth of an ancient gold-working civilisation, haunted the Spanish imagination. 'There had been a golden man, *el dorado*, the gilded one, in what is now Colombia: a chief who once a year rolled in turpentine, was covered with gold dust and then dived into a lake. But the tribe of the golden man had been conquered a generation before Columbus came to the New World. It was an Indian memory that the Spaniards pursued; and the memory was confused with the legend, among jungle Indians, of the Peru the Spaniards had already conquered.'[16] The myth was both a dream and a fever shaping and infecting the lives of Spanish and English, of Antonio de Berrio Walter Raleigh. Naipaul's stripped and lissom narrative follows with meticulous fidelity and urbane restraint the increasingly frantic line of an action conducted in real historical time on real ground, frequently over thousands of real dead bodies, the purpose of which was grossly unreal. It is the discrepancy between the actual explorations, the savage hunting down of the indigenous people, the treacheries, the miniature wars, the marching and counter-marching, the limitless suffering and fatigue on the one hand, and the insubstantial fantasy for the sake of which it was all endured, on the other, which Naipaul's lucid disentangling of events forces on the reader, insisting implacably as it does so on man's (not just Berrio's and Raleigh's) profound, despair-inducing irrationality.

The design, like the pace, the firm characterisation, the rendering of the material tractable to the theme, evinces a mature novelist's skill. It falls into two chiming and contrasting phases; the second, two hundred years later than the El Dorado episode, recounts how the British unblushingly undertook a highly ambiguous operation to organise a revolution in the Spanish Empire on the highest principles of liberty and law, at the same time as they were establishing in Trinidad a slave colony. In this morally clouded context, in a country where the English merchants drank what they were used to in England, claret, madeira and port, and the Negroes died young from overwork, bad food and special Negro diseases like *mal d'estomac* caused by dirt-eating, in this province of Spanish artisans and French and British immigrants, looked upon by the resident officials as 'the scum and sediment of the West Indies, or insolvent shopkeepers and adventurers from Liverpool and Lancaster', where the last Indians lived in alcoholic ennui in their mission-reserves, the central figures are the British Governor, General Picton, and the expatriate South

American, Francisco Miranda. General Picton, who was to die a hero at Waterloo at the age of 56, was 'a rough foul-mouthed devil as ever lived' according to Wellington. He was 38, a Welshman of obscure origin 'bred among the goats' his subordinates said, quick-tempered, red-faced, over six feet tall. He ruled Trinidad like an eighteenth-century Indian nabob. His enemies claimed that he had made his fortune by hunting down runaway Negroes and selling them again; he supplied his estates with stock and timber and salt fish by illegal barter with United States ships. He gathered in fees, the recognised way for a Governor to make a living, levied on everything from the selling of slaves to the playing of billiards (every billiard table in Port of Spain paid Picton sixteen dollars a month), something like 12,000 dollars a year. He himself, a Negro-owning tyrant, lived under the tyranny of a mulatto, Rosetta Smith, in Government House.

The event which ruined Picton's private empire in this ghost province was his authorisation of an act of horror which was nevertheless no more than routine in that time and place. The chief magistrate was examining Louisa Calderon about a possible theft, and he brought to Government House a torture order: 'Appliquez la question à Louisa Calderon. Apply the torture to Louisa Calderon.' Picton signed it. Out of this grew the scandal that his enemies in Trinidad and London seized on to force a Government enquiry and his eventual dismissal. It signalled also the final conclusion of the efforts of Miranda, the son of an immigrant Caracas draper, looked on in England as a Latin aristocrat and highly respected for his political insight and skill, to persuade the British Government to supply the resources for an attack on Spanish possessions. Miranda was a man in love with the idea of British liberty and moved by the ideal of bringing this new, explosive force to bear upon a repressive Spanish tyranny. Miranda's personal life was a pose, but his spirit was disinterested and his courage and pertinacity endless. It was an accident that he did not become a force in history. He had hoped for a British liberation of South America, but the British wanted a conquest and were prepared to support him only as an instrument in that design. When this no longer had any validity, when it began to be clear that the centre of British imperial power would move from America to the East, and that Trinidad would never usefully serve as a springboard for an attack on South America, Miranda 'the man of action who had always had bad luck and had always bungled action' accompanied Trinidad in its fall from history. 'The slave islands in the West were seen to be run down, Port of Spain was once again [to become] a remote municipality.' Miranda, says Naipaul, had a sense of the deeper colonial deprivation, the sense of the missing real world, and it was the deprivation which Miranda felt in his own time that was to become for Naipaul the permanent condition of Trinidad itself.

3 Major Phase, I

Naipaul's masterpiece, *A House for Mr. Biswas*, was published early in his career in 1961 in his thirtieth year. It is a novel in the grand manner, deliberate, large in scope, constructing a world with authoritative ease, with a central figure, a biographical line, a multitude of grasped minor characters, people seen from within so that they possess an intrinsic, spontaneous vitality, and from without, so that they are located in time and place and in a context of value and feeling. The distaste for certain aspects of humanity, faint in his earlier work, harsher in the discursive books and in his latest novels, is taken up here into a much more inclusive sensibility which is concerned with an essential humanity and which blends unsentimental accuracy in notation with a braced pity and tensed, athletic tolerance. It is a novel which has, too, a more profound value, a deep poetic truth. This is realised in the creative, encompassing metaphor which initiates and sustains the novel. At the root of that metaphor is the idea of slavery. Naipaul had mentioned in an earlier book, *The Middle Passage*, the difficulty of finding in Trinidad physical evidence of slavery. But that palpable absence of external institution does not mean that slavery had not inflicted an incurable wound on the national consciousness. The members of the community in *A House for Mr. Biswas*, even those like the Indians who were exempt from formal, historical slavery, carry about with them in their attitude and posture, in their management of life and feeling, the indelible mark of the slave, who is supremely the unnecessary man. All are impelled by the urgency to demonstrate, to themselves even more than to others, their human necessity. In the earlier novels they did this by bruising themselves absurdly and ineffectively against an indifferent universe. Mr. Biswas constructs the proof of his necessity in both a comic and a most moving way. Saturated as he is with the ethos of the given place, maltreated by

its peculiar deficiencies and cruelties, he is none the less realised
with such complete conviction, so living a reality, that he becomes a model of man, just as the history and situation which
formed him are seen to be a metaphor of the process which
constitutes any man.

If one says that *A House for Mr. Biswas* is a traditional novel,
one is not thereby asserting that it is fastened in some disabling
way in nineteenth-century fiction, or that it is oblivious, or incompetent in the use of, technical 'advances'. It is to say that the
novel is free from pinching anxiety about pressing into service
technique for its own sake or for the sake of fashion. The fiction
creates a world, peoples it, shapes its progress; the author speaks
when he feels he has to, mildly or incisively or pityingly but always
appropriately. He feels under no necessity to take a vow of silence
or to pretend that he is not actively engaged in creating his own
work. If he seems to know all—to be what is referred to dis-
approvingly by some critics as 'the omniscient author'—if he
makes no bones about his complete awareness, that is because he
is completely aware and because he *is* the omniscient author.
Fiction is not a refinement of *trompe d'oeil*. Technique in this novel
is to be taken on a more serious plane. The contemporaneity of
the novel depends on the vitality of its reaction, not on the
modishness of its form. Naipaul answers positively the question
posed by Leavis. 'Is there any great novelist whose preoccupation
with "form" is not a matter of his responsibility towards a rich
human interest, or complexity of interests, profoundly realised?—
a responsibility involving, of its nature, imaginative sympathy,
moral discrimination and judgment of relative human value?'[1]

The novel begins with Mr. Mohun Biswas, a sacked journalist,
dying at the age of 46 in his irretrievably mortgaged house in
Sikkim Street, St. James, Port of Spain. He is penniless. He has
had months of illness and despair, he has a wife and four children.
And yet he is struck again and again 'by the wonder of being in
his own house, the audacity of it: to walk into his own front gate,
to bar entry to whoever he wished, to close his doors and windows
every night, to hear no noises except those of his family, to wander
freely from room to room and about his yard ...' The key
phrase here is 'to wander freely'. The substance of the novel has
to do with the transformation of Mr. Biswas, a slave to place,

history and biography, into a free man, the sign and realisation of that emancipation being his house. 'How terrible it would have been, at this time, to be without it: to have died among the Tulsis, amid the squalor of that large, disintegrating and indifferent family; to have left Shama and the children among them, in one room; worse, to have lived without even attempting to lay claim to one's portion of the earth; to have lived and died as one had been born, unnecessary and unaccommodated.'

There is a heroic quality in Mr. Biswas's final attainment of necessity and accommodation. That we accept this note in a character so dry, so small and irritable, at the end of a life so soured by defeat, witnesses to the springy, constructive irony which sustains the novel throughout. It is a positive irony of the recognition of possibility in a context of hopelessness—not a corrective or deflationary one. The house stands as a symbol of Mr. Biswas's astounding achievement; its incorrigible seediness is in keeping with Mr. Biswas's temperament and history. The significance of the house was 'stupendous'. But the house itself was a very modest structure to carry such symbolic weight. It was designed by a solicitor's clerk who built houses in his spare time on lots of barely reclaimed swamp from frames found on an abandoned airfield. The staircase was put up as an afterthought, the doors would not open, the windows would not shut. But for Mr. Biswas it was 'a new, ready-made world. He could not quite believe that he had made that world. He could not see why he should have a place in it. And everything by which he was surrounded was examined and rediscovered, with pleasure, surprise, disbelief. Every relationship, every possession.'

Symbols, marked like the house by external discrepancy and inward fit, played their part at both ends of Mr. Biswas's life. He was born to a family of sugar-cane workers at an inauspicious time and the wrong way round, a scrawny, pot-bellied baby with six fingers, one of which fell off when he had hardly yet got under way. The midwife declared, 'whatever you do, this boy will eat up his own mother and father', and the pundit had to use his most extensively disingenuous powers of interpretation to find anything in Mr. Biswas's disastrous horoscope to mitigate the evil he would undoubtedly bring. Even his sneeze was unlucky: threepence would be lost, a bottle would be broken, a dish upset.

His life was to be a succession of mishaps, each designed to make the point that he was necessary to no one and dependent on everyone. His dependence was not simply the appealing dependence of the helpless which had to be protected, but that of a property, a thing to be possessed. His family disintegrated when his father, supposing him to be drowned (although Mr. Biswas had been warned to stay away from water, which was unlucky for him) dived after him again and again, and finally failed to come up.

The society (with the history implicit in it) which would produce the wiry, flinching figure of Mr. Biswas (and having done so coldly demonstrate his superfluousness) is evoked with humour for its absurdity, sadness for its cruelty, and precision in everything. This capacity for definition which is also embodiment, for solid and refined denotation, lies at the heart of Naipaul's expressive power. His mind and his language work, not by any poetic murmuration or suggestiveness, but by pointing, by specifying, delimiting, detailing. To arrive at the utmost clarity is Naipaul's artistic purpose; to mark off the detail in its uniqueness, whether it be object or feeling or event, is his method. The details so defined are assembled with such unobtrusive tact, with such a fine sense of what is sufficient, that without display or excess or strain, they make a composition lit by a level and equal light, as convincing and as self-endorsing as a natural substance.

As a child, Mr. Biswas was small, thin, with two huge eyes outlined in black and scored with scabs and sores and the marks of eczema: a nervous apology of a child. During the next ten years he became a trifle less nervous, a degree more robust. He was put to school, after a birth certificate had been fudged up and his existence therefore publicly guaranteed, to the ferocious Lal, where between floggings and recitals of *ought oughts are ought, ought twos are ought*, he learned to say the Lord's Prayer in Hindi, made copious notes about geysers, rift valleys, watersheds and currents, got as far as Simple Interest and learned to turn dollars and cents into pounds, shillings and pence; he lived for eight months in the scrubbed house at pundit Jairan's, where he was sent to learn a spiritual profession, perhaps because of the curious air of disaster he carried about with him, and where he wasn't flogged but was treated with abstract and high-minded cruelty; he worked in a rum shop dedicated to sodden drinking and he was sacked by the querulous manager who suspected him of being a spy of the owners. Mr. Biswas was not a graceful victim; there was nothing grand or stoic about him. A thin grit of mutiny was sprinkled through his personality. He mocked the schoolmaster when it was safe to do so and he revenged himself on the manager of the rum shop by spitting in the rum when he bottled it every morning. (The rum was the same: but the prices and names were different, 'Indian Maiden', 'White Cock', 'Parakeet'.) He became a sign writer and he found satisfaction in controlling the brush and flattening the stroke into clean, true curves. It was satisfying work but irregular, and nothing qualified his uneasiness at being a floating particle of being, who was owned by whoever employed him but belonged to no one. It was while painting signs in a shop belonging to the Tulsis, a kind of Hindu Mafia, whose house was decorated with a statue of the benevolent monkey god Hanuman, that Mr. Biswas formally and explicitly entered into the state of slavery.

Mr. Biswas was enlisted into the retinue of the Tulsi clan when he made a clumsy advance to a pretty Tulsi girl, but this faint disturbance at the edge of the web was enough to get him involved in it for the next ten years of his life. Before he knew where he was, he was accepted as the girl's official suitor and before he could understand what that meant he found himself married to her. He was not only naturally a slave, but officially one. The Tulsi family condensed into itself the character of the larger world outside. It was fundamentally indifferent but grasping. It ran on superstition and power, expressed in the Tulsi case in the mysterious matriarch and in her brother-in-law the gangsterish, overpowering Mr. Seth. Its system was to provide subsistence and cover in return for total devotion and the abdication of self. Its modes of behaviour were derived from a remote civilisation— from India—but they were merely forms, empty of any content of value. Everybody lived at Hanuman House in a complex net of relationships and transient alliances, the purpose of which was to placate the authorities and to slide through life unnoticed. In this cruel, comic world, both crowded and solitary, bullying and servile, Mr. Biswas kept alive a mere glint of independence and self by refusing to be either a suave or a mild victim. He was weak but he nourished his querulousness and kept his malice going.

When it was necessary to be solemn he was a clown, when pious he was blasphemous, when he was supposed to be appreciative he was ungrateful.

Mr. Biswas's harassed, factious life with the Tulsis, combining Byzantine intrigue, palace precedence and the smell of bedbugs and kerosene (the kerosene would not kill the bedbugs but it would keep them quiet for a while), is constructed with cleanliness and assurance and Naipaul's characteristic lucidity of line. Mr. Biswas's resistance to total absorption in the Tulsis, his will to keep open a gap between him and the clan, takes a variety of forms. Sometimes there would be odd spurts of external rebellion. At other times, when he was working in the shop where he had been installed by the Tulsis, when they could no longer put up with him in the house, he would devote himself to some absurdity for a whole week, growing his nails to an extreme length, holding them up to startle customers, picking and squeezing at his face until his cheeks and forehead were inflamed and the rims of his lips were like welts. Or he would devote himself to an internal independence and cultivate his mind. He would paint, cool, ordered forest scenes rather than the rotting, mosquito-infested jungle he could find around him. Or he would read, with a despairing aspiration towards the redemption of style, Marcus Aurelius or Epictetus. Mr. Biswas was horribly incompetent in the shop, cheated and despised by his customers and frequently deserted by his wife, who returned every so often to Hanuman House. He had innumerable bad debts and once again the Tulsis had to intervene to protect their interest.

> Seth sighed. 'So what we going to do with the shop?'
> Mr. Biswas shrugged.
> 'Insure and burn?' Seth said, making it one word:
> *Insuranburn.*

After Seth's fire and the collection of the insurance, Mr. Biswas himself receiving seventy-five dollars, he was despatched, a utensil from which some further use might well be squeezed, as a sub-overseer to a sugar estate at Green Vale, at twenty-five dollars a month. He lived in a barracks and his early sympathy for the labourers turned to sour disgust that they should be getting as much as they did. On their side, with the infallible nose of the victimised for the more victimised, and with the cruelty of those who if they have nothing else have stability, they mocked and persecuted him. It is in this phase of the novel that we see at its most refined the psychological acumen for which all of Naipaul's work is so notable, a form of analysis which is also a revelation of a unique individual and the clarification of a universal process. The account of Mr. Biswas's dissolution is both clinical and evocative, accurate and pitying. Mr. Biswas's senses are strangely heightened. He developed odd, compulsive habits: he bathed incessantly; sometimes without being fatigued he found he could do nothing but lie on his bed and read the newspapers the wall was decorated with. He found himself repeating meaningless and irritating words. The gap between Mr. Biswas and the objective world, which he had tried desperately to preserve as some assurance of his own existence, began to open up inside himself. The objectivity he resisted began to invade him: 'but now in the shape and position of everything around him, the trees, the furniture even those letters he had made with brush and ink, there was an alertness, an expectancy.' Objects lost their neutrality and substituted a complicated menace for their simple presence.

The crumpling self made his relationships with others, and particularly with his wife, intolerable. Everything tasted of fear: 'every man and woman he saw, even at a distance, gave him a twist of panic'. Each day his period of lucidity lessened. 'Between the beginning of a routine action and the questioning the time of calm grew less. Between the meeting of a familiar person and the questioning there was less and less of ease. Until there was no lucidity at all, and all action was irrelevant and futile.' He clung tormentedly to his idea of the house. He found a site and a builder, Mr. McLean the carpenter, who began to raise a queer, square structure for him. But while the wretched house assumed its form the handful of Mr. Biswas's sanity dribbled away. He became simply a crumpled object flung among other objects. His life was composed of panic, compulsion, inaction, despair. He slept with a cutlass. He filled his room with intricately ornamented placards. Each act, however minute, became something absolute and undismissible.

He finally existed as a point of terror in a thicket of enmity. He felt darkness lapping about him; in fact the place itself was losing definition; people were becoming remote and faceless, an over-whelming but formless threat:

> When he got to Green Vale it was dark. Under the
> trees it was night. The sounds from the barracks were
> assertive and isolated one from the other: snatches of
> talk, the sound of frying, a shout, the cry of a child:
> sounds thrown up at the starlit sky from a place that
> was nowhere, a dot on the map of the island, which was
> a dot on the map of the world. The dead trees ringed
> the barracks, a wall of flawless black.[2]

I have abstracted the theme of Mr. Biswas's mental collapse to illustrate Naipaul's sense of the rhythms of the human mind, in this case of the disintegrating mind. But I should not want to leave the impression that it can be detached from, or that it is in any way isolated within, the novel. It exists there as a strand, admittedly one carrying a central, tonic value, in an intricately knitted pattern. The theme of Mr. Biswas's deterioration, like the figure of Mr. Biswas himself, exists in a world which has volume and weight at every point. This faculty of Naipaul's unerringly to pursue a specific line without over-emphasising it or manipulating it into an undue prominence is contributed to by a number of other skills. In particular there is the talent I have referred to before, the talent for the choice and accumulation of detail: his ability to give to the most glancingly present of minor characters, fulness and weight; his consciousness of social complexity, and of the historical dimension which supports it; and, finally, and par-ticularly in this novel, the maturity of an attitude which is balanced, comprehensive and without illusion.

Here, for example, are two representative passages from this part of the novel which show his creative use of detail. In the first one, while the remorseless activity of the ants confirms the existence of a world of inhuman ferocity, the writing itself is in-formed simultaneously by the hysterical intensity of Mr. Biswas as he stares at the scene:

> A fresh cycle of rain started. A winged ant dropped
> on Anand's arm. Hurriedly he brushed it off; where the
> ant touched him seemed to burn. Then he saw that the

room was full of these ants enjoying the last minutes
of their short life. Their small wings, strained by large
bodies, quickly became useless, and without wings they
were without defence. They kept on dropping. Their
enemies had already discovered them. On one wall, in
the shadow of the reflector of the oil lamp, Anand saw
a column of black ants. They were not the crazy ants,
thin frivolous creatures who scattered at the slightest
disturbance; they were the biting ants, smaller, thicker,
neater, purple-black with a dull shine, moving slowly
and in strict formation, as solemn and stately as
undertakers. Lightning lit up the room again and
Anand saw the column of biting ants stretched
diagonally across two walls: a roundabout route, but
they had their reasons.[3]

The second passage occurs at a point in the novel immediately
succeeding Mr. Biswas's crack-up. In it we are reminded of the
climate and the physical quality of the world Mr. Biswas belongs
to, while we also become conscious of the hint of a new beginning
not only for the day but also for Mr. Biswas:

Towards the middle of the morning the sky lightened
and lifted, the rain thinned to a drizzle, then stopped
altogether. The clouds rolled back, the sky was suddenly
blinding blue and there were shadows on the water.
Rapidly, their gurgling soon lost in the awakening
everyday din, canals subsided, leaving a wash of twigs
and dirt on the road. In yards, against fences, there
were tidemarks of debris and pebbles which looked as
though they had been washed and sifted; around stones
dirt had been washed away; green leaves that had been
torn down were partly buried in silt. Roads and roofs
dried, steaming, areas of dryness spreading out swiftly,
like ink on a blotter. And presently roads and yards
were dry, except for the depressions where water had
collected. Heat nibbled at their edges, until even the
depressions failed to reflect the blue sky. And the
world was dry again, except for the mud in the
shelter of trees.[4]

As for the second 'skill' on my list, this could be verified from the most random turning of the pages of the novel. One simply takes it for granted in reading the book: takes 'it' and thereby silently benefits from a communication which is never thin and verbal but constantly grounded and endorsed. It may be done by a comment on character or a note on physiognomy or a remark on posture. The result is to enliven every corner of the book and to leave nothing which is not vibrant with presence. Here are two tiny notations which make the point: the first on Mr. Biswas's grandfather who appears once for a moment: 'Bipti's father, futile with asthma, propped himself up on his string bed and said, as he always did on unhappy occasions, "Fate. There is nothing we can do about it." No one paid him any attention. Fate had brought him from India to the sugar-estate, aged him quickly and left him to die in a crumbling mud hut in the swamplands: yet he spoke of Fate often and affectionately, as though, merely by surviving, he had been particularly favoured';[5] the second, the midwife who appears even more fleetingly: 'The midwife, an old, thin, inscrutable Madrassi, came to the hall and sat on her haunches in a corner, smoking, silent, her eyes bright.'

Mr. Biswas's return from the 'wall of flawless black' to a daylight consciousness, stumbling and backsliding as it was, took place in the city of Port of Spain, where, with one short break, he was to spend the next fifteen years of his life. The elaboration of this subject composes the second half of the novel, and it is in the course of my discussion of this that I hope to refer to the third and fourth items of my catalogue of Naipaul's novelist's skills, a sense of society and a comprehensive humanity of attitude to his material and to life. That the city should be the scene of Mr. Biswas's recovery is nicely fitted to the nature of his disease. This was a condition caused by the crumpling of self in the face of external opposition or the collapse of self into the status of an object—an object owned by another. For one smothered in the claustrophobic air of the Tulsis, the city with its openness and impersonality was refreshing and invigorating. Its complex structure and the routines which fascinated Mr. Biswas, its astringently indifferent citizenry—like the beggars lounging about the bandstand so confident about their appearance that they disdained to beg—offered to the damaged soul that measure of detachment

39

and peace within which it could begin to heal itself. Mr. Biswas's affliction was one in which at certain times objects, of which he was one, became poised in a trance-like immobility, any threat to which ravelled him with anxiety:

> As he concentrated, every object acquired a solidity, a permanence. That marble-topped table with the china cup and saucer and spoon: no other arrangement of those objects was possible. He knew that this order was threatened; he had a feeling of expectation and unease. [6]

The mutability of the city, the succession of its moods, its complexity of classes, places, institutions, its range of habits, the whole intricate organisation, enchanted Mr. Biswas, helping him to see the continuity persisting through change, and removing from the phenomenon of alteration the terror of disintegration. At the same time the palpable evidence of an impersonal past in stone, tree, shop, street, as well as its insistent immediate influence in the wet cinema posters, the crowded pavements and the continuous traffic, in the railway station, in the fretworked doors and the fern-smothered verandas, helped him to forgive his own past:

> The past could not be ignored; it was never counterfeit; he carried it within himself. If there was a place for him, it was one that had already been hollowed out by time, by everything he had lived through, however imperfect, makeshift and cheating. [7]

Place hollowed out by time, the past carried within the person: Naipaul's double insight brings to the portrait of Trinidadian society, vivacious and minutely particularised as it is, the extra thickness of an historical background. It is in this more completely rounded, more established world that Mr. Biswas climbs the final gradient of his life. It is not an uninterruptedly smooth progress. There are frantic moments when he seems to be sliding hopelessly backwards into disaster. But Mr. Biswas has a balancing measure of luck during his convalescent period. The family is re-united, his son is bright and sturdily independent, his daughter amiable, his wife reconciled. He is allowed to rent a relatively luxurious Tulsi house in Port of Spain. He finds a job which gives him both pleasure and dignity. The buffoonery and reading which maddened the Tulsis in his earlier life appeal to the editor of a ramshackle, disreputable paper in the city, and Mr. Biswas makes his provisional appointment secure with a ludicrous feature about an explorer's journey, called *Daddy Comes Home in a Coffin.*

The blend of fantasy and clowning shown in Mr. Biswas's news-paper pieces goes with a new insouciance of temperament, capable now of enjoying itself because it is in possession of itself. Once in the Tulsi home 'claimed by no one, he had reflected on the un-reality of his life, and had wished to make a mark on the wall as proof of his existence. Now he needed no such proof. Relation-ships had been created where none existed; he stood at their centre.' It is this re-centring of the displaced impulse and the re-structuring of self which follows on it which are elaborated in the long second half of the novel with unvarying and disciplined lucidity. It is worked out in a nest of family relationships, in his work as a journalist and a social worker, and amid the racial, rural, urban pressures of the larger Trinidadian society. It is a picture which in its fullness takes in man's frailty, corruptibility and viciousness, while it recognises the modest pretensions of hope and the possi-bility, if not the promise, of reconciliation. As a composition, manifold in scope, packed with detail, its design shaped round the principal subject, it calls up the remarks of Henry James about his great story *The Coxon Fund*: '. . . the main merit and sign is the effort to do the complicated thing with a strong . . . luci-dity—to arrive on behalf of the multiplicity, at a certain science of control.'[8]

The complicated thing, the strong lucidity, the science of con-trol: how apt James's phrases are to the subject of Naipaul's theme and to the clarity and certainty with which it is realised. One influence making for this result is the proportion subsisting between the novelist's constitutive insight—man in or resisting the condition of slavery—between this on the one hand, and the image of this condition, the house and the search for accommoda-tion, on the other. Mr. Biswas's pursuit of habitation is the inti-mate and universal expression of man's effort to humanise his context. The house is a shelter, a fortress, a declaration of inde-pendence, a shaping of the impersonal in the service of the personal. Certainly in Mr. Biswas's life it was the effort to become an accommodated man which nourished his most profoundly human aspirations. It was the sense of the loss of his house as part of the dribbling away of his small, clutched store of certainties which signalled as a young child the inauguration of his servitude. It was lodgings like the one with the pundit which forced on him a feeling of external possession. It was life in the barracks of Green Vale which prepared his breakdown, the hopeless occupation of Mr. Maclean's botched construction which utterly brought him down. His recovery began during his semi-independent occupation of the rented house—the rent being his wife's labour—in Port of Spain, and was completed in his own, even if heavily mortgaged, house in the short time before his death.

A House for Mr. Biswas is a novel which is both large and strict. Space is the mark of a work which covers some fifty years in time, climbs and descends a long ladder of experience and stretches across the whole face of a society; control, the conscious direction and the fine management of detail and theme, is the method of the author. Space and control are in a more intimate sense intrinsic to the substance of the novel: space, its definition and possession and necessity, is the initiating impulse of Mr. Biswas's growth; substituting control over space for its passive occupation is the decisive activity of his life. In the end it is by the filling of space with his own human concern that he achieves not simply the control but the creation of his own identity. He becomes a householder instead of a hired hand, a permanent settler instead of one of those intense, transient but somehow servile presences that flash about the earlier books.

I have referred in the course of my discussion to Naipaul's mastery of detail, to the shaped solidity of his minor characters, to his analytic sense of society. The other quality is the comprehensive humanity of the author's attitude. In his first books Naipaul looks at the characters and their world from a distance. He understands them perfectly of course. His defining technique is such that there is no haze around the edges, no puzzling knot in the middle. All—all that is necessary to his purpose, that is—lies open to his calm intelligent scrutiny. But the writing gives the impression that the characters share only a limited part of the author's nature. They exist as elements in a composition (which of course they are) inward, vivid, vital but lacking what James called 'the freedom of the subject'. There is a minor, subservient quality in them, the product of Naipaul's self-contained detachment. It is a reflection surely, this plastic manipulable quality, of the author's near-clinical detachment. In *The Middle Passage* and *An Area of Darkness* disillusion with the past, horror at the present, and what personal bitterness we do not know, helped this separating distance to harden into distaste, revulsion and even despair. *A House for Mr. Biswas* is free both of the butterfly-watching stance of the earliest work and the despairing verdict on mankind which begins to sound in the later. Sparing nothing in judgment, hedging neither in representation nor reaction, the whole matter of the novel is yet informed with a fullness of human sympathy. The deficiencies, the pretensions and cruelties of the society Mr. Biswas is embedded in are recorded as effects of our common humanity, not as the operations of an alien or inferior nature. Mr. Biswas himself, twisted, difficult, intermittently crazy as he is, is projected in all his seedy uniqueness, such is the combined force of Naipaul's communicating skill and inclusiveness of view—yes, but as a fellow sufferer, as a brother not a freak. And as a brother, one feels, not just to us but to Naipaul himself, who is, surely, for all the India-hating response in his *Area of Darkness*, profoundly Indian in the nature of his sensibility. If it is the Brahmin in Naipaul's nature which makes him flinch at the flesh and its corruptibility, it is the comprehensiveness of the Indian with his absorptive generosity and tolerant genius which reconciles in this novel so much that is coarse, disordered and graceless, those elements in existence most deeply antagonistic to the bias of Naipaul's sensibility.

Sometimes in Naipaul's work the reader has the sense of the cool eye of a well-bred stranger analysing with superlative acuity some smothering, medieval strangeness; one has the sense of a most intelligent and gifted member of one species probing and cataloguing the weaknesses of quite another. But not in *A House for Mr. Biswas*. The relationship of author and subject, in part the connection of Naipaul and Mr. Biswas himself, is one which exists on a level, as between equals. Mr. Biswas is felt and suffered with, not just seen and suffered. This mild and charitable acceptance, this capacity to unfold without smudging or distaste, shows itself at every point in the novel, and as clearly as anywhere in the muted, curbed conclusion.

How different from the rich normality of *A House for Mr. Biswas* is the menacing fairytale *Mr. Stone and the Knights Companion* (1963), Naipaul's first novel with a wholly English setting. The strangeness does not come from any unfamiliarity with the locale, the Englishry of which is solid and accurate. The 62-year-old Mr. Stone, a librarian in a large firm, his house, his lumpish housekeeper-char, Miss Millington, his office routine, the details of English suburban life, the pepper dust for the cats, the jealousies of the neighbours, the mild snobbery, the social competition, all have a grounded and unmistakable reality. They are reported by an eye which notes both the surface and the assumptions waving cloudily beneath it, but it does so without any fatigue of unsurprised expectation. Each ripple of the routine glistens with novelty. Mr. Stone is not only a creature of, but a slave to, habit. The greatest of habits is the past and Mr. Stone cultivates and reverences it—his own past, that is. He never rushed a performance of any habitual duty; 'experiences were not to be enjoyed at the actual moment, pleasure in them came only when they had been, as it were, docketed and put away in the file of the past, when they had become part of his "life", his "experiences", his career. It was only then that they acquired colour, just as colour came truly to nature only in a coloured snapshot or a painting, which annihilated colourless, distorting space.'

But the period during which the past was neutral and its passing not a cause for alarm was dribbling away from Mr. Stone. Mr. Stone, for most of his life flinching from even the faintest suggestion of the unorthodox, began as he raced towards retirement (from the office? from life?) to be harassed by intimations of mortality. We accept this metaphysical note in so dry a character because Mr. Stone had always enjoyed a secret, fantastical life, and because his complex humanity is fully established by the author. This neat person, who is in the habit in moments of solitude of writing out tabulated accounts of his career, relished grotesque fantasies, 'He thought of moving pavements . . . He was able to fly. He ignored traffic lights; he flew from pavement to pavement over people and cars and buses (the people flown over looking up in wonder while he floated serenely past, indifferent to their stupe-faction). Seated in his armchair, he flew up and down the corridors of his office.'[9]

He noticed one day a London Transport poster which announced 'a trip to London's countryside . . . will reassure those who doubt the coming of Spring'. It was Mr. Stone's doubt about the coming of Spring, his sense of a relaxing hold on life, which brought both a personal and professional revolution into it. He married, a queer, creaky but not unsuccessful marriage, and his great creative idea came to him. He persuaded his chief in the firm to set up the organisation of Knights whose chivalrous duty was to visit and comfort the retired. This was Mr. Stone's stroke against an existence hardening on the one side into routine and on the other into despair.

There is a touch of sweetness in the recognised possibility of subdued romance in so unrefreshed and waterless a life as Mr. Stone's—evidence of increasing complexity in the author's attitude—and there is further proof of his impressive range in the success in which the wild folk-gaiety of the earliest books modulates into the elegant, urban comedy of this one. But the lightness and delicacy of the fantasy cannot disguise a fundamental seriousness verging on the grim. There is comfort for Mr. Stone, just as there is a suggestion of hope for the reader, but this is not to be gained, in Naipaul's vision of life, by refusing to see that all that matters is man's own frailty and corruptibility, that the order of the universe, to which he seeks to align himself, is not his order. 'And he had a realisation,' it is said of Mr. Stone, 'too upsetting to be more than momentarily examined, that all that was solid and immutable and enduring about the world, all to which man linked himself . . . flattered only to deceive. For all that was not flesh was irrelevant to man, and all that was important was man's own flesh, his weakness and corruptibility.'

The difference between *A House for Mr. Biswas* and *Mr. Stone and the Knights Companion* is not merely that between a major and minor work, though it *is* that; it is also a difference in theme, shape and interest of a kind which suggests something of the range of Naipaul's ability. His volume of short stories, *A Flag on the Island*, shows how extensive is the stretch of his capacity. As a register of experience *A Flag on the Island* includes the ambivalent

*

relation of a boy to his working mother, 'The Enemy'; a night watchman's diary of his frantic night-time's work, 'The Night Watchman's Occurrence Book'; the comic ironies implicit in the assumptions about the differences of race, 'The Baker's Story'; a rich boy's impelled cruelty to his dog, 'The Heart'; the lyrical lunacy of a religious aunt, 'My Aunt Gold Teeth'; the intimate venom of a houseful of lodgers, 'The Perfect Tenants'; the superficiality of self-regarding suffering, 'The Mourners'; the innocent and terrifying paranoia of a converted Hindu schoolmaster, 'A Christmas Story'; a drama of the life of caged birds, 'Greenie and Yellow'; and the reversal of experience caught in a wartime soldier's return to the West Indies, 'A Flag on the Island'. The variety of subject is matched by a variety of mood, of tone, of treatment, of point of view. Naipaul has the essential gift of the short story writer: he is a manager of implication, a writer who is capable of raising a world upon the slim foundation of a handful of characters, each of which is established with hardly more than a verbal flick or gesture and the minimum of setting and space. What is not said counts as much as what is; silence is expressive; the interstices of action matter. In 'My Aunt Gold Teeth', the first story in *A Flag on the Island*, the lightness of tone and the kindness of attitude are proportioned to the material of a tale in which the extreme of eccentricity is seen as part of the absurdity of reality rather than the extravagance of farce. In the same way the narrative voice is buoyant and casual, addressed conversationally to the reader, and able to incorporate without jarring or artifice a range of folk speech, sly, allusive, wry, proverbial, deadpan.

> I never knew her real name and it is quite likely that she did have one, though I never heard her called anything but Gold Teeth. She did, indeed, have gold teeth. She had sixteen of them. She had married early and she had married well, and shortly after her marriage she exchanged her perfectly sound teeth for gold ones, to announce to the world that her husband was a man of substance.[10]

Into this off-hand beginning is insinuated the whole development, the authentic character and confirming setting of the crazy but human aunt who, while convinced that Hindus were the best people in the world, and that Hinduism was the superior religion, while half fearing her husband's Brahminical flair for clairvoyance, yet sidles about surreptitiously shopping for the practices of other religions. In the same way we see in the first sentence of 'The Raffle'—'They don't pay primary school teachers a lot in Trinidad, but they allow them to beat their pupils as much as they want'—the conventional brutality of an alien educational system, just as we are aware in the first words of 'A Christmas Story'— 'Though it is Christmas Eve my mind is not on Christmas'—the dislocation of attitude at the centre of a helpless, driving madness.

Naipaul's short story technique is a matter of elucidating what is concealed in the beginning. One says 'elucidating' because his is a wholly rational art which does not permit the writer any indulgence in the discourse of dreams, or any lapse into tranced talk below the level of consciousness, even when the subject is a powerfully realised paranoia. Not that he offers anything like 'rationalist' explanations in the narrow sense for the conduct or the personal mysteries of his characters. But however opaque or inexplicable the action, it is presented with an unblurred exactitude and bathed in the light of consciousness. In any case the world, the human not just the West Indian world, supporting and producing his characters, is one in which the unexpected, the sudden sideways jump from the orthodox, is an essential part of experience. It is a universe where meaning is not exhausted by the enumeration of antecedent causes. So many cultures, such differences in racial temperament, so interwoven a tissue of historical influences, meet in this society that everything is open and changeable, and surprise a constituent of any event.

The pair of stories with an English setting in *A Flag on the Island*, 'Greenie and Yellow' and 'The Perfect Tenants', shows a double and opposed capacity. On the one hand everything is seen as strange and fascinating, observed, as V. S. Pritchett says, 'with a foreign eye', or, in the words I quoted earlier from Naipaul himself, all are seen as 'adepts in a ritual the traveller doesn't know; . . . moving from one mystery to another'. On the other hand, the British reader cannot but be struck by the clear authenticity of each shade and nuance of lower middle class suburban life. The effect is of something utterly new and unfatigued and yet totally recognisable, creating what Henry James called in his preface to the *Aspern Papers*, 'an annexed but independent world.' How fresh and true, for example, in 'Greenie and Yellow', that unsentimental, diminutive drama of the caged birds, is the mere catalogue of the cage's furniture:

> The cage, when I had seen it in the basement window, was an elegant little thing with blue bars to match Bluey's feathers, two toy trapezes, a seed-trough, a water-trough and a spring door. Now every Friday there were additions: Mrs. Cooksey shopped on Friday. The first addition was a toy ferris wheel in multicoloured plastic. The second was a seed-bell; it tinkled when Bluey pecked at it. The third was a small round mirror. Just when it seemed that these additions were going to leave little room for Bluey, Mrs. Cooksey added something else. She said it was a friend for Bluey. The friend was a red-beaked chicken emerging from a neatly serrated shell, all in plastic and weighted at the bottom to stay upright.[11]

Or how both newly noted and faithful to the spirit of the place and the manners of the house is the compliment paid by the landlady to her perfect tenants: 'They're very fussy.' Or how self-validating and yet how original the list of the possessions of another couple of tenants, those from the flat below dressed in their tweedy sub-county manner and looking constrained and unhappy, including

> contemporary coffee tables . . . a 1946 Anglia which at the appropriate season carried a sticker: FREE LIFT TO GLYNDEBOURNE AT YOUR OWN RISK.

Naipaul's imagination is much engaged with two human experiences which are at once familiar and ultimate, that is with presence and absence: a theme, I remind myself, that preoccupied Coleridge in his great poem, 'This Lime-Tree Bower My Prison'; and it is also, I feel, not extravagantly inappropriate to point out that the structure of Coleridge's poem, the immediate present burrowing into the past and then hinting at the shape of the future, is identical with that implicit in the most substantial piece in this volume, the title story, 'A Flag on the Island'. In it a middle-aged American returns to the island he knew as a war-time soldier. He goes back accidentally, when the ship he is travel-ling in is diverted by a hurricane, and, reluctantly, since, as he notes, it is 'so easy to destroy more than a name. All landscapes are in the end only in the imagination; to be faced with the reality is to start again.'[12]

There are three movements in the composition, the present when he leaves the ship and makes a bemused round of the island, now the possessor of its own flag when it once had only the remote affirmation of the Union Jack and the precise contempor-ary signal of the U.S. Army. This frantic and intoxicated first period fines down to the place at which he first came to know, and become part of, the island, to the point at which the land-scape of memory, of imagination, takes over from that of reality and the confusion and threat of fact. The revival of this past experience—the second phase—is the substance of the story and it shows Naipaul's powers at their most sensitively mature. The area is so confined, the treatment so intense and the procedure so effective in revealing time, layer by layer, that one seems to be taking part in the skilled excavation of a narrow site, the result of which is life and presence rather than history and archaeology. It leads irresistibly in the third section to the hopeless shabbiness of the future.

The second phase of the story, then, begins after the blurred tour of the island when the returned soldier suddenly decides to make for the place he knew when young. His feelings flow imme-diately into those he felt on his first walk to this place, and we see how the memory is used as the creative instrument not just for recovering but for constructing the past. There is a dislocating contrast between the moment of revelation in this first walk and the near-pentecostal fear which accompanies it, and the simple ordinariness of the place, which is simply known as Henry's place. '. . . The Coconut Grove, the wind blowing my hair, making my shirt flap, and it seemed that it was just in this way, though not at night and under a wild sky, that I had first come to this street. The terror of sky and trees, the force at my feet.'[13]

49

Henry's place, indistinguishable from the shabby neighbouring houses and the backyards, and next door to the Premier Commercial College, whose principal H. J. Blackwhite taught shorthand and book-keeping and wrote romantic novels in his spare time, was a club, a meeting place, a haven, a place of assignation. It is in fact an image, miniature and lucid, of the island itself. It had no commercial organisation, just as the island itself had no organisation. 'This place,' said Mr. Blackwhite, 'I tell you is nowhere. It doesn't exist. People are just born here.' It was like 'a carnival or a sports meeting held on a race day or a cricket or football match: . . . and you must picture it going on, with lots of other sporting activities taking place at the same time, each activity unrelated to any other, creating a total effect of multi-farious frenzy . . .' without a past or stability or pride. Those who resort to Henry's place are first, living against a huge absence, the abolished past, and secondly, distinguished in the same way as the characters in the early stories, by their genius for individuality, like Henry himself or Mr. Blackwhite the writer, or the tall bearded Priest, later, as Priestman, to be a successful television personality, and by the wit and grace of their manners and speech. They are people with style. 'I always like hearing a man use language well' says the girl, Selma, of Priest, and this is a disposition shared by all and in fact a capacity all are equipped with, whether of the formal kind when they are positively Victorian, or of the informal sort when language becomes a kind of jazz of the streets.

In this world girls move from relationship to relationship, fearing marriage because marriage was a means of quick degradation. The mild and amiable Selma, between whom and the soldier exists a genuine feeling, felt that 'once she surrendered completely to one man, she lost her hold on him and her beauty was useless, a wasted gift'. The code of life was total freedom and complete non-responsibility, characteristics we see in the literary and educational life of Mr. Blackwhite, in the blend of religion and obeah, in the vigorous prosecution of the blackmarket in stolen U.S. goods and the strenuous selling of insurance, the buying of which had now a social cachet. This seething yard, pullulating with human individuality, connects sadness and comedy in an unbroken line. For all the vitality and the limpid gaiety, the sense of human loss and frustration informs everything. But the gaiety, on the other hand, is of a pure and jewelled kind. Here, for example, is Henry's account of his own background:

'I will tell you, you know,' Henry said. 'When the old queen pass on—'

'The old queen?'

'My mother. I was in a sort of daze. Then I had this little dream. The old man, he appear to me.'

'Your father Hezekiah?'

'No. God. He say, "Henry, surround yourself with love, but avoid vice." On this island I was telling you about, pretty if I tell you, they had this woman, pretty but malevolent. She make two-three children for me, and bam, you know what, she want to rush me into marriage.'

The sun was going down. From the base, the bit of tropics we had created, the bugle sounded Retreat. Henry snapped his fingers, urging us all to stand. We stood up and saluted to the end.

'I like these little customs,' he said. 'Is a nice little custom you boys bring with you.'

'About this woman on the pretty island with two or three children?'

Henry said, 'I avoided vice. I ran like hell. I get the rumour spread that I dead. I suppose I am dead in a way. Can't go back to my pretty little island. Oh, prettier than this. Pretty, pretty. But she waiting for me.'[14]

Or here is how the community, the motto of which according to Henry is 'We all have to corporate in some way. Some people corporate in one way, some corporate another way', 'corporate' with one another and the police in a raid:

A whistle blew. There were cries of 'Police!' and in an instant the yard was transformed. Dustbins appeared upright here and there; liquor bottles disappeared inside some; the dancers and the audience

> sat in neat rows under the shed and one man stood at
> the blackboard, writing. Many of Henry's girls put on
> spectacles. One or two carried pieces of embroidery.
>
> It seemed to me that the police were a long time in
> entering. When they did, the Inspector shook Henry by
> the hand and said, 'The old Adult Education class,
> eh?'
>
> 'As you see,' Henry said. 'Each one teach one.'[15]

Not one of these short stories, grim or gay, but gains from
Naipaul's unerring touch for the socially significant trait or action
or turn of phrase. How much, for example, about education in
the island, its arrangements, its hollowness, is conveyed by that
phrase, 'the old Education Class'. How clearly the diary of events
in 'The Night Watchman's Occurrence Book' indicates the pointless, frenzied self-indulgence of the rootless and of the tourists in
the island. How much of the meaning of lower middle-class
suburban life in London, with all its mummified ritual and its
almost religious sense of social prestige is caught in the business
of the uncollected milk bottles on the doorstep in 'The Perfect
Tenants'. How clearly again that special, effortless and somehow
justified Chinese self-containment is present in the remarks on
Ma-Ho's children in 'A Flag on the Island':

> His children remained distinctive, and separate from
> the life of the street: a small neat crocodile, each child
> armed with neat bags and neat pencil boxes, going
> coolly off to school in the morning and returning just
> as coolly in the afternoon, as though nothing had
> touched them during the whole day, or caused them to
> be sullied. In the morning the back door of his shop
> opened to let out these children; in the afternoon the
> back door opened to swallow them in again; and nothing
> more was heard from then, and nothing more was seen
> of them.[16]

These precise notations of group habit and manner, support
and exemplify Naipaul's sense of the movement of social process.
Change in 'A Flag on the Island' is a silent, invisible but chronic

condition. The island society with its hollow past and its weakness in internal resource is peculiarly open to infection. The American presence and the American black market carry with them as well as charity and illicit goods the other values of American life. A varnish of Americanism slowly covers the individuality of the island. Mr. Blackwhite, the romantic, becomes a fashionable black writer courted by the agents of charitable foundations, Henry's place becomes the Coconut Grove, Priest becomes Gary Priestland the T.V. star, Ma-Ho's children become girls in frilly short skirts singing commercial jingles for a local rum.

The works I have spoken of in this chapter demonstrate the height of Naipaul's art together with its extent and variety. The suppleness of the treatment, the fastidious detachment, the independence of stance, the freedom from anything merely fashionable, the nervously inward sympathy with character, the limpid style, the purity of the insight, the imaginative richness and inventiveness and the disciplined pity are marks of an authentic and original talent of a very distinguished kind. These qualities are nourished by and progressively realise in the fiction a restrained and coherent, almost a classical attitude towards human nature, which blends in equal proportions a recognition of its manifold variety with a sense of its intrinsic limitation, its frailty and corruptibility. Part of that attitude is the awareness of some stubborn discrepancy in existence by which life limps on and on long after it has reached its point of perfection. 'I feel the world need this sort of thing every now and then. A clean break, a fresh start. But the damn world don't end. And we don't dead at the right time.'

4   Major Phase, II

It is from this very insight, life outliving its point, that *The Mimic Men*, published in 1967, powerfully takes off. It brings together West Indian and British themes and sets alongside one another the landscapes of London and Trinidad, or Isabella, as the island is called in the story. It is a more intimately personal work than *Mr. Stone and the Knights Companion*, which gives a rather careful, 'studied' impression. It is like *A House for Mr. Biswas* in its complexity and inclusiveness but the temperament of *The Mimic Men* is grimmer and gloomier. *A House for Mr. Biswas* celebrates the fineness of humanity implicit in the feeblest of us. The more contemplative eye of *The Mimic Men* observes the failure in the best, like the worn little pornographic booklet discovered in the desk of the hero's father. There are splendid comic touches, as always, but they are dispersed and rare. The hilarity of the early novels, in which indeed there was sometimes a note of desperation, has now turned into something bordering on despair, and all that quality of wild high spirits is quite bleached away. *The Mimic Men* begins with Ralph Singh, an exiled, or rather a withdrawn politician, fatigued by disillusion rather than failure, writing his memoirs in an aseptic, placeless London suburb. The novel dramatises his reminiscences. The framing effect of the reminiscences, the distancing of exile and the sieve of memory, give a kind of remoteness to the novel's form and enable us to grasp the quality of detachment in the protagonist, just as they also remind us of that contemplative constituent in Naipaul's own sensibility which assumes a more important place in his fiction.

The action swirls back and forward in a rhythm that follows the starts and turns of memory. But there is one insistent theme, the pursuit of order, and one recurrent image, the image of landscape, both real and ideal, which informs the varied material of Ralph Singh's life with an inward and poetic unity. It is in rela-

54

tion to the search for order, and by the tactful use of a method of imagery, that the character of the hero is revealed to the reader. There is no tumultuous or violent modification of that development. It is rather the elaboration, the solidifying, of a given bias. What he was as a child he more and more becomes as a man. The brilliant idler at Isabella Imperial School becomes during his irregular, promiscuous life in a college off the Aldwych, 'the dandy, the extravagant colonial, indifferent to scholarship'. It was a part which others, like his playmates at school and his mistress-housekeeper Lieni, encouraged him in, and since 'we become what we see of ourselves in the eyes of others' he acted the rôle convincingly. But the glittering and careless amateur, which at the time he felt himself simply to be playing, was not expressing a merely non-existent side of himself. 'As though we ever play. As though the personality, for all its byways and wilful deviousness, all its seeming inconsistencies, does not hang together.' He had tried in London to find an order, an extension of himself, and to hasten this process had given himself a personality. But this adopted personality was truer to himself in a deeper way. It spoke for a certain icy remoteness in his being, an incapacity to melt away into relationships with others. The lightness of touch, the wit in action he showed to others, was really a profound indifference to them, the gay and amiable creature was in fact expressing a profound disdain. London, a city of miraculous light, had been his emblem of order, solid, central, connected with the past. But it was an ideal which, for all its beauty, failed him. 'All landscapes eventually turn to land, the gold of the imagination to the lead of the reality.' He felt in the city at moments of self-awareness what he had felt from childhood onwards, that he was 'spectral, disintegrating, pointless, fluid'.

> The city made by man but passed out of his control:
> breakdown the negative reaction, activity the positive:
> opposite but equal aspects of an accommodation to a
> sense of place which, like memory, when grown acute,
> becomes a source of pain.[1]

A sense of place which becomes a source of pain: this was something Ralph Singh was born to. He remembered as a

55

schoolboy the saying of an ancient Greek that the first requisite for happiness was to be born in a famous city but 'to be born on an island like Isabella, an obscure New World transplantation, second-hand and barbarous, was to be born to disorder'. The portrait of Singh, each stroke of which is clean and sharp but which in totality appears as richly and subtly worked, shows him as an instinctive aristocrat, for all his poor schoolmaster father and his mother with her vague connections with wealth in the form of a relationship with the owners of the Coca-Cola bottling plant on the island, whose life was spent attempting to construct or to discover the order his nature so acutely felt the absence of. He was also a man marked by an icy remoteness since childhood. An intellectual and moral distance persisted between him and any other person and he was also, therefore, a man impelled by hollowness and cold to seek substance and warmth. This double deficiency of situation and temperament he attempts to remedy by his move to London, another society, another place, and by pursuing there with the cunning and perseverance of an addict the most chaotic kind of sex.

The two themes of London and sex are brilliantly elaborated by Naipaul in a composition which, however complicated in its detail, has a strong lucidity in its design. London is seen as a series of marvellously recreated landscapes, exercises in varieties of light, gradually failing in its capacity to satisfy the imagination. Sex becomes a succession of unrelated adventures in which, indeed, the constitutional detachment from human connection of the protagonist becomes even more set and contemptuous. One girl will turn out to have 'a back of irritating coarseness'; another will have a skin which smells. 'There were bumps and scratches, there were a dozen little things that could positively enrage me.' Intimacy began to be a horrifying word, a form of self-violation. The emotional incapacity and the aristocratic disdain feed one another 'but the restlessness remains. It took me to innumerable tainted rooms, with drawn curtains and bedspreads suggesting other warm bodies. And once, more quickening of self-disgust than any other thing, I had a sight of the prostitute's supper, peasant food, on a bare table in a back room.' For such a man relief was both intolerable and impossible: the city an idea to be pursued in vain, sex a form of private rage.

A keen symmetry of pattern takes Singh, now married to a gritty north London undergraduate, back to the island of Isabella where he explores two other routes towards relief. The remedies here, nicely corresponding to the city and the sex of his London life, are wealth and politics. The four themes flow in and out, succeeding, displacing and overtaking one another in time, in emphasis and importance. Wealth came to him almost accidentally as the consequence of exploiting an apparently worthless property he had been left. He and his wife are dazzled to be among the rich. He did not feel responsible for the fortune which had befallen him. 'I always felt separate from what I did.' This grossness of wealth, of possessions, of women, drinks, swimming-pools, restaurants, airports, provided neither ease for his sense of distance nor any form of order acceptable to a sensitive and cultivated man. He and his wife are happiest outside in a crowd with the champagne working and communication reduced to contact. The gift of wealth proved to be an intolerable burden.

The achievement of order through the pursuit of political power is the theme of the middle and active part of Singh's life, the phase he was later to call the parenthesis. This, the most original part of the novel, communicates with strength and depth the protagonist's sense of outward participation and inward absence, or to put it as it appears to him, of a façade of public illusion concealing whatever he experienced of personal reality. Singh's political rôle had been prepared for by his antecedents, by his mother's connection with wealth, and by his father's sudden assumption in late middle age of a crazed messianic rôle as the leader of the deprived in the island, in a movement which spread like fire among the poor. '. . . for all the emblems and phrases of Christianity that he used, it was a type of Hinduism that he expounded, a mixture of acceptance and revolt, despair and action, a mixture of the mad and the logical. He offered something to many people; but it was his example and his presence rather than his teaching which mattered.' But of course it could not endure, being no more than 'a gesture, a mass protest, a statement of despair, without a philosophy or cause.' Its effect on Singh's life was to attach a vaguely political nimbus to the family. As significant for his political life was his schoolboy friendship with Browne, who was to become the leader of the Negroes. And of course the time was right, the context in which a man like Singh could become a successful politician was establishing itself. Naipaul's account of this process, not at all abstract, oblique and wholly immersed in the fiction as it is, has a large and luminous air about it, a sense of great social movement, the unlocking of immense stabilities, of something which is in part a secret, insensible development and in part a sudden, absolute, geological shift of forces. Naipaul's comprehension of large-scale change is accompanied by a precise feeling for the exact tang of the sensibility of revolution. On the one side there was the decline of imperial power and confidence, the realignment of classes and races within the island society, on the other the insatiable appetite for change and a justified sense of oppression. Moreover, there were like Browne, but unlike Singh, politicians with 'the frenzy, the necessary hurt,' as well as those who were simply 'chap-men in causes.' This frenzy and hurt were what alone made politics real. Without these they became for Singh a set of dream-like motions performed by an intruder in a society in which people were linked by no internal connection. The flinching distaste for human intimacy evident in Singh's sex life in London is mirrored in the hauteur he felt, and did not always succeed in disguising, towards the whole class of politicians. Later in London, after this active parenthesis, he spoke with distaste of the English politician he found when he came to England at a time of reform '. . . politicians proclaim the meanness of their birth and the poverty of their upbringing and describe themselves with virtuous rage as barefoot boys. On Isabella, where we had the genuine article in abundance, this was a common term of schoolboy abuse; and I was embarrassed on behalf of these great men.' The contempt explicit here tainted all his relationships with politicians on the island—it is the political face of his fundamental isolation—the formidable and enigmatic Browne apart.

The development of these two lines, Singh's relationship with Browne and the rise of the new men, is a fine example of the novelist's art, the two strands plaited together with the lightest, deftest skill, so that the result is a composition which is both an evocation and an analysis. Singh's boyhood attachment to Browne at Isabella Imperial School was tense and burdensome, since Singh was surrounded by an aura of the well-bred and the wealthy even if his family situation was comparatively modest, and Browne was a bright boy with a family embarrassingly proletarian to an upper-class schoolboy. The relationship was kept alive by glancing contacts in London and Isabella which are placed in the action with unassuming, tactful naturalness. The association becomes alive and positive when the course of colonial history, the displacement of the metropolitan power, the consciousness of race, together with the inadequacy of the current politicians, mere contractors and merchants in the towns, farmers in the country, without any policy but themselves—when all these things prepare a state of affairs ready for manipulation by those with the resources and intellect to question the very system itself. 'Simply by coming forward—Browne and myself and *The Socialist*, all together—we put an end to the old order. It was like that.'

In these circumstances Browne's *persona*, his status as renegade and romantic, as a radical for whose acknowledged gifts the pattern provided no outlet, and Singh's as the young, cultivated millionaire, together made an irresistible combination. They supported one another and appeared as a portent no one could dismiss. They supported one another in a more intimate way, too. The African with his lacerated and uncertain personality 'needing alien witness to prove his reality', found in the Asiatic Singh a complete person and an unfractured psyche. Singh was presented by Browne with a picture of himself which it reassured him to study. Singh was disturbed by the dim knowledge that this involved his being 'committed to a whole new mythology, dark and alien, committed to a series of interiors I never wanted to enter . . . Joe Louis, Haile Selassie, Jesus . . . the distaste and alarm of boyhood rose up strongly'.

Their bruised and ambiguous relationship in which genuine sympathy was intermittently distorted by the distaste and alarm of boyhood is beautifully executed. A comparable skill appears in the subtly handled development of the political movement headed by Browne and Singh, Browne the prophet and messiah, Singh the regulator of finances and organisation. Their instrument was a newspaper called *The Socialist* and the movement was officially left wing. It stood for the dignity of the working class, the dignity of the distressed, the dignity of the island. But all this was a matter of feeling rather than doctrine, of borrowed phrases and

escape from thought. It included a genuine core of indignation—
to be more and more wrapped round and finally lost—and much
histrionic projection of the same feeling. This attitudinising,
Singh reflects, is a necessary condition of politics since the politician is a man, dealing with abstractions, lifted out of himself
and separated from his own personality. But the personality
offered by Singh—held out to be looked at, almost—was immensely
useful to Browne in the movement, as Browne himself realised
at the start: 'the rich man with a certain name who had put
himself on the side of the poor, who appeared to have been
suddenly given a glimpse of the truth: I was now aware of his
attractiveness. So in unlikely circumstances the London dandy
was resurrected. I knew the affection and kindly mockery he
aroused, and it was pleasant in those early days just to be this
self. I had known nothing like it.'[2]

What was happening in Isabella was happening tumultuously
in twenty different colonies and territories. Singh sees it not as the
pace of post-war political change, neither the pace of creation nor
destruction, but the pace of chaos on which strict limits had been
imposed. And what the movement offered above all was drama—
a sense of an explosion of life and the composition of a pattern of
justice. The marks of success increased: the public meetings, the
tours of dusty country roads, the lengthening reports of speeches,
the policemen in heavy serge shorts becoming less aggressive and
more protecting, the atmosphere of dedication and mutual loyalty
There was also the vanity of those who believed they had the
power to regulate what they had created, together with wonder
at the suddenly realised concept of the people who responded
and could be manipulated. The speeches became more brilliant
and more dishonest, the success more dazzling, the sense of inevitable historical process more certain and finally, election night—
the sobering moment of triumph, when play-acting turns out to
be serious. And then the anxious concern with legality and ritual
to consecrate power, and the realisation that power needed a
more solid base than applause and the smell of the people's
sweat. Finally there was the manœuvring, corrupt or passionate,
to hang on to this airy gift which might at any moment be withdrawn. But in Singh, underneath the public dandy, underneath
the political mover and organiser there was only a negation. The

one prize of politics for him was that he had helped to bring drama to the island. 'Drama, however much we fear it, sharpens our perception of the world, gives us some sense of ourselves, makes us actors, gives point and sometimes glory to each day. It alters a drab landscape.' When the drama failed the landscape returned to its drabness and the images of disorder to his imagination.

> My sense of drama failed. This to me was the true
> loss. For four years drama had supported me; now,
> abruptly, drama failed. It was a private loss; thoughts
> of irresponsibility or duty dwindled, became absurd.
> I struggled to keep drama alive, for its replacement
> was despair: the vision of a boy walking on an endless,
> desolate beach, between vegetation living, rotting,
> collapsed, and a mindless, living sea.[3]

Singh retires from politics and from island life at the age of forty into personal anonymity and an almost 'placeless' situation in a conclusion which links the end of the novel to its beginning. This cyclic pattern seems to be in keeping with the essentially Indian quality of Naipaul's sensibility which, for all his explicit and wholesale rejection of India in *An Area of Darkness*, saturates his work. It is certainly in keeping with the Indian bias of Singh's temperament. He withdraws from unnecessary responsibility and attachment, he simplifies his life and frees himself from one cycle of events. 'It gives me joy to find that in so doing I have also fulfilled the four-fold division of life prescribed by our Aryan ancestors. I have been student, householder and man of affairs, recluse.' Singh's life had been the attempt to impose an order upon the various areas of his experience. Politics had been the effort to impose it upon a society in disarray, his marriage upon his promiscuous emotional life. In this final phase his aim is to impose order on his own life, to make it 'historical and manageable'. The bleak aftermath of Singh's public life, and the empty context of the suburban London hotel, provide him in the composition of his memoirs with the chance to discover the pattern and significance of his life. There are several places in the book where he regards human personality as simply the answer to clues and suggestions offered by others but now he sees his own nature, and the nature of all his political colleagues, his friends and relations, as something very much more *given*.

> As I write, my own view of my action alters. I have
> said that my marriage and the political career which
> succeeded it and seemed to flow from it, all that active
> part of my life, occurred in a sort of parenthesis. I
> used to feel they were aberrations, whimsical, arbitrary
> acts which in some way got out of control. But now,
> with a feeling of waste and regret for opportunities
> missed, I begin to question this. I doubt whether any
> action, above a certain level, is ever wholly arbitrary
> or whimsical or dishonest. I question now whether the
> personality is manufactured by the vision of others.
> The personality hangs together. It is one and indivisible.[4]

He comes, indeed, to share the view offered by R. K. Narayan, in whom the Indian sensibility is so much clearer, purer and simpler than in Naipaul. Singh accepts the truth noted by Narayan in *The English Teacher* that 'a profound and unmitigated loneliness is the only truth of life'.

The essential aim of Singh's life had been to make the enlargement of himself which was his experience more truly coherent with his own nature. He had always failed, as a student, as a millionaire, as a politician. Alone in his London hotel and through the discipline of contemplation '. . . this became my aim: from the central fact of this setting, my presence in this city which I have known as student, politician, and now as refugee-immigrant, to impose order on my own history'. Singh's character becomes one and organic because of the strict honesty which finally controls the relationship between himself and his experience, or because self in him is rigorously educated to become accessible to what is authentically his own experience. This painfully achieved coherence of the character is communicated by a narrative technique which is dissolving and non-linear, in correspondence with the starts and swerves of the recovering memory, his instrument of self-examination. As the reader finds his way through this intricate novel he sees not only the central reconstruction of a subtle and melancholy spirit but the brilliant treatment too of other themes: the violation of colonial society, the seediness and danger which it leaves behind; the psychology of human growth; the rendering of political struggle; the evocation of place and physical context, the London light, the cocoa valley; all informed by the unity of a constitutive theme, the exploration in a conscious individual of modes of mediation between human character and human experience. The novel is the product of an independent, fastidious talent, lithe in its imaginative vitality and penetrating in its intelligent grasp of the subtleties of human feeling. It exhibits a whole constellation of gifts, of analysis, of evocation, of social understanding, of general composition and suppleness of tone. There are weaknesses: a certain limpness or passivity in Ralph Singh himself at key junctures in his life which leave him more puzzling than the reader is willing to accept; the character of Browne as it is drawn in the novel hardly warrants the influence the author attributes to him; the women in the book, with the exception of the wife Sandra, are not treated with Naipaul's characteristically tense energy. But these flaws can be carried by a structure as strong and lucid as *The Mimic Men*.

At this point I have to make some general remarks before, or as, I turn to Naipaul's latest work *In A Free State* (1971). On the last page of *The Mimic Men*, where Naipaul is speaking of Singh's effort to control the chaos of his life by submitting it to the discipline of writing, he says: 'So writing, for all its initial distortion, clarifies, and even becomes a process of life.' Singh himself, I have suggested already, seems peculiarly close in temperament and attitude to Naipaul the writer. But however that may be, this statement is an apt note on Naipaul's own work, which combines in an extraordinary way detachment from the object of scrutiny with a deep engagement of the most personal kind on the part of the author himself, as well, of course, as the most sunlit clarity in the final effect. Next one notes that Singh had retired to a faceless London suburb run dry of character, emptied of uniqueness. This was a function of his final detachment but it is also a signal of how profoundly significant *place* was to him at the beginning of his process of withdrawal. Distress about the place he sprang from turned to despair both about the place itself and any possible surrogates for it, and in the end to indifference. Naipaul himself explains that his early life was deeply disturbed by 'a sense of being in a wrong place'.[5] Writing itself was a way of leaving the wrong place and a mode of enquiring whether there was any right place. One feels now that he, like Singh, has arrived at a point of detachment from this anxiety. Again the reader is bound to discern in all of Naipaul's major novels, the presence of a generative and richly suggestive image which acts at once as the initiator, the embodiment and a commentary upon, the deepest theme of the work. In *A House for Mr. Biswas* it is the house itself and the implied sense of man as a slave, as an unnecessary and unaccommodated creature. In *The Mimic Men* it is the landscape of Isabella and London and the whole conception of place as the proper context of man. In *In A Free State* it is the image of the journey, the movement from one place to another and of what is involved in that, the victimisation, the being alien and lost, the significance of the passage between departure and arrival.

Writing as clarification, as part of the process of life and as an extension of experience itself, is beautifully illustrated in the very structure of *In A Free State*. It begins and ends with extracts from the journal, or rather work-book of the author himself, and takes in three episodes, one in which an Indian servant is transplanted from Bombay to Washington, another in which two West Indian brothers are moved to London, and a third in which an English man and an English woman travel, or flee, through an African country. Each of these episodes is a journey, and journeying means exemption from the customary tether of place, habit and association, putting the traveller in a situation in which he is peculiarly exposed and at risk, and also peculiarly accessible to the discerning eye. The episodes are discriminated one from another by a marked variety of place and person, but there is a deep thematic unity working through them, a perfect homogeneity of subject and attitude, a quality established and reinforced by the mobile and elegantly disciplined narrative line. The themes of journeying and displacement, the act of cruelty, the condition of terror, the dissolution of inward as well as outward peace, the analogy with life itself: these notes are touched lightly in the opening episode and more fully elaborated in those that follow.

The events in 'The Tramp at Piraeus', a prologue which is an extract from the journal—if such a mere snatch of action, such a solitary, extracted incident can be so called—take place on a dingy Greek steamer between Piraeus and Alexandria. They are observed by Naipaul, *spectator ab extra* even more than usual, and written up as part of a professional exercise, part of his writer's daily practice, but also because they constitute one of Henry James's 'germs',[6] 'the single small seed from which a story springs'. The ship is carrying uprooted Egyptian Greeks 'who by simple skills had made themselves only just less poor than Egyptians', the casualties of the new Egyptian freedom, as well as Lebanese, American students, Spanish night club dancers, and fat Egyptian students returning from Germany. They all witness an act of calculated cruelty directed at a crazy English tramp, 'an old man, with a tremulous worn face and wet blue eyes'. In the evenly distributed light of Naipaul's understanding of charac-ter and his sense of context, the object becomes translucent, flinching and naked before the eye of the beholder, and of his surrogate, the reader.

The old man concentrates in himself the lost, hopeless feeling of the transported but since unlike them he is protected neither by rationality nor cunning, and with his spasmodic, repellent ways, not even by the capacity to provoke pity, he is at once a fit victim for the Lebanese, the Austrian, the Egyptian, and the elected scapegoat of all who remain passive in the face of his persecution. The muted fear of everyone becomes in the old man a limitless terror. The author's own fear of becoming involved with him makes clear Naipaul's sense of the continuity of human conduct, since this puts those—including Naipaul—who are only one degree less vulnerable than the old man, in the camp of the oppressors and aligns them with the very forces they are fleeing from.

'Hate oppression; fear the oppressed', is what the politician Singh advised in *The Mimic Men*. The fear of the oppressed in 'The Tramp at Piraeus' hardly rises to anything so active as hate of oppression or of anything else. The inertia not just of self-protection but of a despairing view of human kind is all this fear produces. But Naipaul's sensitivity to distribution and contrast is evident in his placing next to 'The Tramp at Piraeus', 'One out of Many', in which a servant from Bombay is taken by his diplo-matic master to Washington. It is profoundly sad but at the same time nimble and comic. In Bombay Santosh had been to Western eyes little more than a slave, although neither he nor his master saw himself as such. He had a position, he was a member of society, he had his comforts, even his privileges:

> I was so happy in Bombay. I was respected, I had a
> certain position. I worked for an important man. The
> highest in the land came to our bachelor chambers
> and enjoyed my food and showered compliments on me.
> I also had my friends. We met in the evenings on the
> pavement below the gallery of our chambers. Some of
> us, like the tailor's bearer and myself, were domestics
> who lived in the street. The others were people who
> came to that bit of pavement to sleep. Respectable
> people: we didn't encourage riff-raff. [7]

At first he was appalled that he might be left behind, when his master left for his American post, to return to his village in the hills, to his wife and children, to be no more than a porter touting at stations among fifty others. But he goes to Washington in the end with his affectionate master and the various terrors his extraction from his own world submits him to are constructed with a brilliant, unpushing certainty: the horrors of the aeroplane flight; the incomprehensible lavatories; the weird food and the contemptuous company; the continuous enclosure in hissing, air-conditioned buildings; the corridors: the doors; the illuminated ceilings; and then the alien inhabitants themselves, the wild and terrifying *hubshi* and the strange Americans.

> The effect of all this television on me was curious. If
> by some chance I saw an American on the street I
> tried to fit him or her into the commercials; and I felt
> I had caught the person in an interval between his
> television duties. So to some extent Americans have
> remained to me, as people not quite real, as people
> temporarily absent from television. [8]

He escapes from his employer into service in an Indian restaurant. But that break-out imprisons him in the American legal system. He escapes by marrying a Negress. That jails him in a world where everything is strange, the smells, the language, the people. Extracted from his natural context, where indeed he is a kind of slave, he discovers escape itself to be only a different route to a harder kind of slavery. The final stage is total solitariness, something more hopeless than resignation, quieter than despair:

> I am a simple man who decided to act and see for
> himself, and it is as though I have had several lives. I
> do not wish to add to these. Some afternoons I walk
> to the circle with the fountain. I see the dancers but
> they are separated from me as by glass. Once, when
> there were rumours of new burnings, someone scrawled
> in white paint on the pavement outside my house:
> *Soul Brother*. I understand the words; but I feel, brother
> to what or to whom? I was once part of the flow,
> never thinking of myself as a presence. Then I looked
> in the mirror and decided to be free. All that my
> freedom has brought me is the knowledge that I have
> a face and have a body, that I must feed this body and
> clothe this body for a certain number of years. Then
> it will be over.[9]

To move from the mild, even if melancholy air of 'One out of Many' to 'Tell me Who to Kill' is to journey into a more acrid, nerve-racked terrain, in which a young West Indian working man with a hysterical attachment to his brighter, and worthless, brother, works himself to the bone in London after having suffered agonies on his behalf at home. The piece is a study in hatred, a hatred which is the effect of a deep wound in the nature of the protagonist and of a world incapable of healing it. This is true of the world he came from because of its shabby meanness and the absence of any impersonal generosity of standard, as it is of the English world he moved to because of its indifference, hostility and inhumanity. The brother, Dayo, has ascended to the ambiguous status of symbol, and is therefore exempt from the protagonist's view of what constitutes reality, every element of which provokes his loathing, although at the end when the brother is encountered in the real world at his

marriage, when he is seen to be what he is, an idler and a con-
man, he too falls under the jurisdiction of hatred. The paranoic
self-destructive quality of the hatred is conveyed with compressed
force, in the images, in the circumstances, in the reflections of the
speaker. When he looks back at his own village he sees it like this:

> . . . I feel I could look down and see that whole village
> in the damp flat lands, the lumpy little pitch road,
> black between the green sugarcane, the ditches with
> the tall grass, the thatched huts, water in the yellow
> yards after rain, and the rusty roof of that one concrete
> house rotting.[10]

London appears in its public aspect as a big wet rubbish dump or
as tall, black iron railings, or in its more private side as the house
he has to live in.

When he throws up his job in the factory, the one place which
in its detachment and efficiency seems to him a haven, he starts a
small roti-and-curry shop where he is harassed by suspicious
officials in tweeds and persecuted by louts who smash the glasses
and bend the cutlery. His own country had left him with no
supporting mythology except a set of film memories and misspelt
stars' names, and a few instinctive repulsions:

> It is the first time I am in a church and I don't like it.
> It is as though they are making me eat beef and
> pork. The flowers and the brass and the old smell and
> the body on the cross make me think of the dead.
> The funny taste is in my mouth, my old nausea, and I
> feel I would vomit if I swallow.[11]

Images of this sort abound. The overwhelming misery of madness and the extremity of one who feels he is an alien everywhere
and in the end is a stranger even to himself, are conveyed in the
images of self-destruction. 'I only know that inside me mash up,
and that the love and danger I carry all this time break and cut,
and my life finish.'

The pieces so far considered are microscopic in their focussed
intensity. 'The Tramp at Piraeus' concentrated on one act of

deliberate cruelty, 'One out of Many' on one man's solitary imprisonment, 'Tell Me Who to Kill' on a single emotion. 'In a Free State' is larger in scope, more cumulative in building its effect, more inclusive in its material. A man and a woman set out to travel by car from an African capital on a long journey to the southern part of the country. There are uneasy mutters of a coup in preparation, a vague sense of menace and violence in the air. Neither Bobby nor Linda is fitted to cope with the danger and the fundamental irrationality of the situation in the country, and each in his way illustrates that essential discrepancy between traveller and terrain—their modish artificiality, in particular, enforcing their inadequacy in these surroundings—which is the condition of a journey of this kind. Bobby is an administrative officer in the central government (he has been running a seminar in the capital), liberal, sensitive, self-centred, a man with a severe mental breakdown in his history, a homosexual of the prowling kind, infatuated with *Africanité* in spite of his years of African service, 'Africa was for Bobby the empty spaces, the safe adventure of long fatiguing drives on open roads, the other Africans, boys built like men.' Linda is small, boyish, showing her age, with a reputation as a man-eater. Their relationship is 'one of those difficult half-relationships with uncertainty rather than suspicion on both sides'. She is tinkling, grateful, apologetic for imposing her company on Bobby.

The title of this episode, 'In A Free State', is less significant in its literal sense of a newly emancipated colony, and more so in the resonance it has as a scientific metaphor. A molecule in a free state, presumably, is freed from gravitational, electrostatic and magnetic forces, in the same way as Naipaul sees the traveller floating away from habit and the usual scene. In associating a homosexual with a man-eating woman, Naipaul also abolishes what would normally be an expected influence in these circumstances, the force of sexual attraction. So that the situation can develop in a wholly free state in which the two protagonists act upon one another purely as persons, emancipated from everything but themselves and the position they are in.

There is a kind of nakedness in the immediacy of the presence of Bobby and Linda, and yet the relationship is managed with such subtlety and restraint that the dialogue, each side of it exquisitely true to the speaker, makes a ballet of thrust and riposte, irony and impetuous blurting, qualification and denial, confession and lies, silence and equivocation. 'Already he and Linda had become travellers together, sensitive to the sights, finding conversation in everything.' At the same time their flight from the capital, a town more Indian-English than African, into the deep African bush, is an image of the hunting of the King by the President's forces, which is going on around them. ('In this country in Africa there was a President and there was also a King. They belonged to different tribes.') We are made aware of this pursuit, again managed with precise control and delicate obliqueness, at critical intervals: by the drone of a helicopter, by the roadblock, by the soldiers mysteriously appearing and disappearing, by the sight of two naked men, chalked white from head to toe, running on the road, by the intimation of ritual horrors occurring in the background, by a message crackling on the radio, by the impression the landscape makes on Bobby and Linda, pointing to a menace, hinting at disaster.

Bobby and Linda are to some degree rational people, he an educated, she a sensible, person, attempting to impose on material and events resistant to it some pattern of reason. Her prejudices, which she sees the weakness of, his progressive convictions about the essential similarity of African and European, become increasingly insufficient to withstand the intensifying mindlessness and rage around them. We see this in the behaviour of the crazy, derelict colonel who keeps the shabby hotel they stop at on the way, in the pack of dogs gone wild in an abandoned town, in the pointless brutality of the soldiers, in the resigned terror of the inhabitants of the forest, the King's tribe. The symmetry of the themes is carried on to the crisis, in which the murder of the King, reported as a fatal car accident, is paralleled by the haphazard beating up of Bobby by a troop of soldiers for no reason that makes sense. There is no logical or pertinent connection between this event and what goes before except a sense that the universe itself is liable at any moment, and above all in the absence of order, to relapse into anger and lunacy.

This lean *nouvelle*, less than 150 pages in length, conveys, as well as the intensely realised relationship of Bobby and Linda, an extraordinarily rich and complicated reading of the country, of its history, of its present and, one feels, of its future. The psychology of the people, the physical terrain, the light, the relics of history, the chaos of a society without intellectual instruments and stripped of its past, are powerfully established. And like all distinguished art, it conveys, too, the irresistible conviction that however local the circumstances, however concrete the situation, however individual the tone and grain, it is the valid and authentic nature of man himself which is embodied here.

The one limitation on the generality, the fullness of grasp, of this strong, original work, is something I can only call an overdeveloped, on occasion even an overwrought, sense of human offensiveness. It corresponds to that flinching distaste for the human skin in *The Mimic Men*. The reader will remember the passage quoted—bumps and scratches, the dozen things that positively enrage; in 'In a Free State' it is a heightened, almost a frantic sensitivity to human smell. The Africans carry smell about them like a dull obscenity '. . . this smell of Africa . . . It is a smell of rotting vegetation and Africans. One is very much like the other . . . The boy was big and he moved briskly, creating little turbulences of stink . . . Timothy, his smell sharp in the light morning, offered the breakfast card . . .' And it isn't by any means merely an African characteristic, 'Bobby was also aware that the Colonel was smelling. He saw that the Colonel's singlet was brown with dirt; he saw dirt in the oily folds of skin on the Colonel's neck.' In Linda's room 'nothing had been disturbed, nothing had changed, only the smell seemed sharper'. 'The soldier pressed his belly against the car door and the smell of his warm khaki mingled with the smell of the sweat from Bobby's open left armpit and his yellow back.' The note is insistent and sometimes shrill. It suggests in the author some radical horror of human flesh. The bias against the ordinary grossness of human beings which is clearly part of Naipaul's sensibility becomes here a rejection of the flesh itself.

If this is weakness, as I think it is, it is also evidence of another, more positive quality of Naipaul's writing. That is his scrupulous honesty in reporting both the facts of the case and his reaction to them. He never fudges a state of affairs or fakes his feelings. He has an eye without prejudice as well as an eye unclouded by fear that he might be prejudiced, a timidity common enough among a number of English writers. The concluding section of *In a Free State*, 'The Circus at Luxor', another entry from his journal, demonstrates his gift of total fidelity to fact and feeling. It is reporting carried to the point of genius in which the notation of event and the registration of response are equal in their honesty and communicated in a style of comparable purity. This time another act of cruelty, but a routine rather than a deliberate one, shatters for a moment the author's, the observer's, fundamental detachment. It takes place at Luxor in the presence of the world, as represented by English students, young Germans, Italian tourists and Chinese members of a visiting circus. The Italian tourists are throwing food to the children and an Egyptian beats them off with a whip as they scramble for it. It is a kind of game, which when it is not wholly disregarded, is accepted even by those who are being whipped. The author tears the whip from the Egyptian's hand. But nothing comes from this spurt of indignation. The children remain where they are and the author lapses into his indifference. Life is not altered in its quality by the moment of drama. Injustice, anger and then indifference are, it seems, the permanent conditions of all our actions. The Chinese visitors make gifts to the ragged waiters of medals turned out from a mould which had lost its sharpness and of pretty coloured postcards of Chinese peonies:

> Peonies, China! So many empires had come here. Not
> far from where we were was the colossus on whose
> shin the Emperor Hadrian had caused to be carved
> verses in praise of himself, to commemorate his visit.
> On the other bank, not far from the Winter Palace, was
> a stone with a rougher Roman inscription marking the
> southern limit of the Empire, defining an area of
> retreat. Now another, more remote empire was
> announcing itself. A medal, a postcard; and all that
> was asked in return was anger and a sense of injustice.[12]

5 An Album of Response

I began this study by quoting Francis Wyndham's account[1] of the disconcerted response of British critics to Naipaul's earliest novels, and in particular to their wit and urbanity, qualities which seemed then (one wonders why) wildly inappropriate in the conditions of post-colonial society. I want to conclude by glancing at a collection of other reactions, British and West Indian, European and Indian, to Naipaul's work. It is a far cry from that early British bewilderment to Francis Wyndham's own response, of which I give two examples, the first of which appeared as a review of *Miguel Street* in 1959, the second written on the publication of *In A Free State* in 1971. (It is interesting, too, to note the coherence and continuity of opinions delivered at more than ten years' distance.)

> Unity of theme, mood, manner and background binds the stories in V. S. Naipaul's *Miguel Street* so tightly together that the collection is almost a novel. The street is in Port of Spain, and Mr. Naipaul takes us from house to house, concentrating on a character here, a situation there, before moving on to the next: a major figure in one episode may fill a subsidiary rôle in another. It is a form well suited to Mr. Naipaul's talent, but I think it should be mentioned that although *Miguel Street* is published after his two novels it was in fact written before them; a reader ignorant of this fact might be forgiven for assuming that Mr. Naipaul had decided to sidestep the problems of design and construction posed by the full-length novel, whereas his development as a writer really indicates an increased attention to these. The discipline of his prose, and the disenchanted but far from irresponsible gaiety of his

point of view, already distinguish him from other novelists dealing with the West Indian scene, most of whom tend to get carried away, in various directions, by the rich opportunities provided by local colour: Mr. Naipaul's sardonic account of the conflicting simplicities and complexities in Trinidad society (with emphasis laid on the Hindu community) is neither turgid nor 'charming'. If he attains the purely technical skill necessary to maintain his enviable poise throughout a more ambitious work (a skill which neither Lamming nor Selvon have yet exhibited, in spite of their other achievements) he will be outstanding indeed. *Miguel Street* is a deeply enjoyable book, filled with people who are eccentrics without being caricatures—people conceived on the grand scale and brought into perfect focus by Mr. Naipaul's measured observation, which combines the qualities of sympathy and detachment. This detachment is so much a part of his literary personality that any modification of it is curiously effective; and such a modification seems to occur in the last story, 'How I left Miguel Street'. Here the narrator, a 'street arab' whose growth to manhood has been suggested throughout, as it were behind the scenes, leaves for England; it is as though the author himself stepped from the wings on to the stage, revealing significance in what has gone before by giving it simultaneously the mystery of nostalgia and the immediacy of a personal experience.[2]

. . . I consider Naipaul the finest living novelist writing in English, and this his most important work since *Mr. Biswas*. His consummate technical mastery of narrative, dialogue and characterisation (seen at its most dazzling in the African episode) enables him to pinpoint an elusive complexity of meaning through a prose style of lucid purity. These gifts are reinforced by a rare, tough moral honesty that establishes *In A Free State* as an original, unsettling work of art.[3]

But while this latter view may be taken as fairly representative of some of the best critical opinion, there are undoubtedly views of another kind, both British and West Indian. Naipaul himself records that he has been rebuked by writers from the West Indies, and notably George Lamming, 'for not paying sufficient attention in my books to non-Indian groups. A confrontation of different communities, he said, was the fundamental West Indian experience. So indeed it is, and increasingly. But to see the attenuation of the culture of my childhood as the result of a dramatic confrontation of opposed worlds would be to distort reality. To me the worlds were juxtaposed and mutually exclusive.'[4] Naipaul's is a characteristically polite rejoinder to the mildest possible interpretation of George Lamming's opinion, which in fact in its harshness and hostility is not untypical of a good deal of West Indian reaction.

> His books can't move beyond a castrated satire; and
> although satire may be a useful element in fiction, no
> important work, comparable to Selvon's can rest
> safely on satire alone. When such a writer is a colonial,
> ashamed of his cultural background and striving like
> mad to prove himself through promotion to the peaks
> of a 'superior' culture whose values are gravely in
> doubt, then satire, like the charge of philistinism, is
> for me nothing more than a refuge. And it is too small
> a refuge for a writer who wishes to be taken seriously.[5]

It is only fair to point out that this comment was written about Naipaul's earliest work. Even so, most readers will be puzzled as to what is meant to be conveyed by 'castrated', except disapproval. Feeble, fumbling, indecisive, unproductive? None of these terms appears even remotely apposite to the work of a novelist whose delicate placing of effect and whose needle-like precision give the impression of a kind of literary acupuncture, and whose substantial body of distinguished work, whose endless inventiveness, leave most of his contemporaries deeply in the shade.

When he uses the word 'satire', however, George Lamming raises a matter which is cogent and interesting, in spite of his appearing to imply that the satirical is not a proper literary motive, and that the literary impulse of West Indian writers should be above all pity and indignation. (In any case, surely it is quite clear that Naipaul's 'satire' or rather his critical habit, has not by any means been preserved simply for the West Indies; England, India, Africa have been its targets too.) The topic has been taken up in a temperate and intelligent way by the young West Indian critic Gordon Rohlehr[6] discussing this very statement of George Lamming's. (Gordon Rohlehr makes the point, incidentally, that 'Naipaul is a Trinidad East Indian who has not come to terms with the Negro-Creole world in Trinidad, or with the East Indian world in Trinidad, or with the greyness of English life, or with life in India itself, where he went in search of his roots.') 'Satire,' Rohlehr writes, 'is the sensitive measure of a society's departure from a norm inherent in itself. Since Naipaul starts with the conviction that such a norm is absent from his society, his task as satirist becomes doubly difficult. Not only must he recreate experience, but also simultaneously create the standards against which this experience is to be judged. This explains the mixture of farce and social consciousness which occurs in the two early novels.'

Later in his essay Gordon Rohlehr makes two other points about Naipaul's irony, one on the added strength he gains from his ironic distance, the other on the limitation implicit in Naipaul's detachment from the West Indian experience. In the first place, he sees that the value of Naipaul's irony is

> that it enables him to examine his past without any
> sentimental self-indulgence. We see Biswas as a full
> human being who is as weak and contemptible as he is
> forceful and admirable. Irony enables Naipaul to get
> down to the bare humanity beneath his history. Because
> he is dealing with his own personal past, his irony does
> not preclude sympathy but reinforces it. He is able to
> answer in terms of creative sensibility a question to
> which he could find no satisfactory academic answer.[7]

Next he wonders at Naipaul's hypersensitivity and asks himself whether the neurosis is completely controlled by the irony. 'Is not this complete aquiescence with Froude that there are "No

people there in the true sense of the word", a formula for evading
the complex sympathy which the West Indian experience seems
to demand?'[8] Rohlehr does not interpret Naipaul's assent to
Froude's view as a snobbish aspiration after 'superior' metropolitan culture in the way that Lamming does, but he sees it as too
easy an adoption of a European reading of history. It is interesting
to put alongside Rohlehr's comment the point which is made, in
much the same context, by another West Indian scholar, G. R.
Coulthard. Coulthard contrasts Naipaul's attitude to the West
Indies with the Cuban writer Alejo Carpentier's to the Latin
American world in general.

> The divergent approaches and reactions of Naipaul on
> the one hand and Alejo Carpentier on the other seem
> to me to be two significantly interesting poles between
> which West Indian culture moves. Between them lie
> a morass of folksy, picturesque and clumsily nationalistic
> work.
>
> Naipaul is an excellent writer in the British tradition,
> who to a large extent has used West Indian subject
> matter, often treated critically through irony and satire,
> but who rejects the West Indies and becomes almost
> comically indignant if anyone calls him a West Indian
> novelist as he thinks that West Indian writers have
> failed in their task 'through reflecting and flattering
> the prejudices of their race or colour groups'.
>
> The Cuban, Alejo Carpentier, while writing as it were
> only incidentally about the West Indies (except in his
> early novel *Ecue-yamba-o* which he now regrets having
> written), is in fact of an infinitely broader cosmopolitan
> culture than Naipaul, but far from rejecting the West
> Indies has widened his scope into the actual concept
> of a distinctive American literature already referred to.
>
> In his *Autobiografía de prisa* he writes:
>> 'My surrealist efforts seemed a vain task to me.
>> I could add nothing new to the movement. I had
>> a hostile reaction. I felt a burning desire to give
>> expression to the American world. I still did not
>> know how, but I was inspired by the difficulty

of the task on account of my ignorance of the real
American essences.'
Carpentier's 'American world' is not only the West
Indies, but the West Indies are very much part of it.[9]

A calmer, more objective literary reason for Naipaul's varied
reputation in Britain and the West Indies is advanced by the
coolest and best equipped of West Indian academic critics,
Kenneth Ramchand. (Not that one should suppose all of Naipaul's
British critics to be all of a piece. For example A. C. Derrick, in
an essay in which the author's distaste for the subject disturbs
the grace of the expression, finds that

> In his satiric presentation of characters Naipaul rarely
> allows himself to show a humane understanding of
> their weaknesses. . . . What is perhaps most unsatisfying
> about the novels set in the 'second-rate' West Indian
> colonies is their final hollowness, their lack of balance.
> It is not simply a matter of Naipaul's having created a
> motley array of failures and ridiculous figures. To some
> extent it results from his characters being judged not
> against attitudes and values existing in their society,
> but against an implicit norm of human tastes and
> behaviour which Naipaul considers desirable and which
> he assumes the reader will approve of. Within the
> fictional world of the novels, however, such a norm is
> denied even a possible existence. There is thus nothing
> to clearly counterpoint the satiric demonstrations of
> the shoddy, the absurd and the ridiculous. The social
> condition itself, with its myriad flaws, is presented as
> fixed and unalterable, and no character ever achieves
> anything worthwhile.)[10]

Ramchand, who sees Naipaul as the most observant and least
metaphysical of West Indian novelists, affirms that in his central
preoccupation he is at odds with most West Indian writers:

> '. . . Living in a borrowed culture, the West Indian,
> more than most, needs writers to tell him who he is and

where he stands.' So writes V. S. Naipaul in *The Middle Passage* (1962). It is not unique for novelists to be regarded as having something special to say to their societies. But the West Indian novelists apply themselves with unusual urgency and unanimity to an analysis and interpretation of their society's ills, including the social and economic deprivation of the majority; the pervasive consciousness of race and colour; the cynicism and uncertainty of the native bourgeoisie in power after independence; the lack of a history to be proud of; and the absence of traditional or settled values. If, however, the social consciousness of writers from the islands draws attention to itself as a peculiarly interesting matter, it is worth suggesting at once that this social consciousness is not class-consciousness. . . . Although West Indian novelists are aware of the main pattern of the nineteenth-century English novel—an analysis of character in relation to the manners and morals operative in a given period—it follows from the formlessness of West Indian society, and the existential position of the individual in it, that such a pattern is not one that seems relevant or comes spontaneously to the writer from the West Indies. This may well be one of the reasons for the higher reputation in Britain than in the West Indies of the Trinidadian V. S. Naipaul (b. 1932), whose deflation of characters by means associated with novels dealing with manners and morals appears to West Indians to be at least extraneous to the same author's expression of the void in colonial society.[11]

Behind the void, however, lurks the ghostly presence of El Dorado, the possible existence of which in the South American heartland has vibrated in man's imagination 'since the days when the conquistadores were hoping to make it the centre of the third and richest province of the Spanish Empire.'[12] The golden world, the subject of Naipaul's *The Loss of El Dorado*, is examined by the Belgian scholar Hena Maes-Jelinek who sees it as an essential element in the experience supporting Naipaul's fiction.

> *The Loss of El Dorado* is not the work of an historian.
> Nor is it a work of fiction, though Naipaul's portrayal
> of real people definitely bears the novelist's stamp, but
> of a novelist for whom human beings are in this
> particular instance either inefficient or bad. However,
> since it is partly an imaginative work, the work of an
> artist rather than a scholar, and one in which the mode
> of presentation is predominantly satirical, its relevance
> to his fiction is obvious: the one complements the other,
> and his description of the past in *The Loss of El Dorado*
> accounts for the picture of Trinidad that emerges
> from his novels. . . . In Naipaul's latest novel, *The Mimic
> Men*, the sense of lost opportunity and wastefulness is
> even more obtrusive. It is a story of disorder at all
> levels, based on fear, the inescapable legacy of the
> slave society which makes people suspicious of one
> another. It corrupts them from their very childhood,
> making them dishonest, irresponsible impersonators
> who perpetuate the island's tradition of inefficiency. . . .
> In spite of Naipaul's restrained and sensitive style *The
> Mimic Men* falls short of his previous achievement
> because the narrator comments on his past and on the
> state of Isabella but does not always bring them to life.
> Even the shipwreck metaphor is explained and not
> worked out in the narrative. But this novel is more
> explicitly than any of his work an exploration of spiritual
> disease in individual and society. The satirical impact
> of Naipaul's fiction is due to the discrepancy between
> men's aspirations and their ineffectual, often comic,
> attempts to achieve them. The vision of an El Dorado
> hopelessly out of reach is always implicit in his novels.
> In retrospect it is even possible to see that all the
> characters of Naipaul's novels form a long gallery of
> 'Mimic Men' whether we think of Ramsumair in *The
> Mystic Masseur*, of Harbans in *The Suffrage of Elvira*, or
> of all those who achieve a fake success in their

second-hand world. When his characters are genuine,
they are inevitably failures, and not even tragic ones
because there can be no tragedy in a society which, in
the author's words, 'denies itself heroes'.[13]

Of all Naipaul's books those which have provoked most comment are a discursive work, *An Area of Darkness*, and his finest
novel, *A House for Mr. Biswas*, and I want to concentrate the
remaining critical comment I have to quote on these two. The
devastating *An Area of Darkness* naturally produced the most
scalded reaction in India. A very mild and well-bred version of
Indian feeling on the volume is offered by Mrs. Nandakumar:

His subsequent visit to India, the land of his remoter
ancestors, was an even more shattering experience to
him, as may be inferred from his recent book, *An Area
of Darkness* (1964). What he saw—or chose to see—was
not what he had expected to see, and he became sullen,
he felt disillusioned. Poor India had not come up to
his expectations (what exactly were they?), and he felt
no hesitation in saying so in so many words. He had
missed the simple fact that India was not Trinidad, nor
England for that matter. The things he saw and recorded
with a tiresome particularity were certainly there, but
there were other things too which his observant eye
shouldn't have missed.[14]

A less accommodating attitude, a more energetically argued re-
buttal of Naipaul's case and a considerable measure of diagnostic
understanding of Naipaul's own problem, are offered by the
vigorous Indian critic, C. D. Narasimhaiah:

It is a tantalising mixture of first-rate literary sensibility
along with what should belong to potboilers, namely,
a morbid obsession with filth, dirt, defecation, and an
extraordinary lack (in one so gifted) of sympathy,
penetration and concern for people as people. . . . *An
Area of Darkness* is too good to be called a mere hit-and-
run kind of traveller's diary and too often obtrusively

personal. . . . Where shall we seek the clue to this
callousness and perversity? *He* of course thinks it is all
in India. . . . 'Somewhere, something has snapped', he
says, of India in history . . . Students of Indian history
know that creativity dried up long ago, we became
repetitive and imitative and we lost the social sense
with increasing gap between the individual and society.
But that is all part of the nation's history, quite beyond
his grasp, and here in this book it is the tragedy of an
extraordinarily gifted, proud, sensitive individual for
whom something has snapped inside and whose book,
therefore if it makes the reader sad, has left the writer
sadder, but not wiser. For it is the agonising experience
of a homeless, rootless man without country, without
religion, without a set of beliefs and values to live by.
For when after this self-laceration in India he goes
back to England emptiness stares him in the face and
emptiness ends in despair.[15]

A more sympathetic acceptance of Naipaul's undertaking in this
volume is exhibited by M. Bryn Davies:

. . . Naipaul's novels about Trinidad deal with a
relatively isolated community which he had been
brought up in. It was still an Indian community with
closely knit family traits, but Indian with a difference,
and in *The Mystic Masseur*, *Mr. Biswas*, and other
novels Naipaul looked back on it with a tolerant blend
of humour and nostalgia which gave the novels their
current appeal. But when Naipaul went to India and
found the Trinidadian squalor and corruption magnified
on the scale of a great nation, the effect on him was
profoundly disturbing. What he related in Trinidad,
with the same ironic semi-humorous detachment as
R. K. Narayan in his chronicles of Malgudi, now
appeared in all its bloated misery and disillusionment;
and to Naipaul at any rate the spiritual assets of India
were not enough to offset the feeling of apathetic
misery and decay.[16]

Perhaps I may be allowed to quote my own response to the work, written on the book's appearance:

> . . . Mr. Naipaul came East, and a cold coming he had of it. He endures within himself Indian agonies. The friction of the two sides of his nature produce not warmth but despair. . . . Although this book shows on every page the novelist's double discernment, which is able to fix the subtlest nuance of individuality, and with an equal assurance, an equal skill, to establish it solidly in a social world, it is valuable very much more as a report, inward and tremblingly exact, of the nature of Naipaul than as an undistorted chronicle of India. Mr. Naipaul's revulsion at so many aspects of Indian life, his almost Swiftian horror of dirt, his novelist's fierce rejection of the Indian sense of non-reality, his suspicion, even his fear, of the way in which the brutality of fact in India can slide away into formless diction— all these things quiver on every page. But they never qualify or muffle his astonishing sense of detail. The book is crammed, exhilaratingly sharpened, by this extreme clarity of vision. . . . Perhaps it is the dissolving of action into being which most appals him. But perhaps there is also something Indian in his fascinated horror with such detail. He is, it seems, rejecting not only India but trying to bleach out part of his own nature. His book is a kind of metaphysical diary of the effort to shine a Western novelist's light into an interior area of darkness. It reconstructs, it doesn't simply record, this experience, and it is deeply, deeply disturbing.[17]

Finally, here is a set of views about what is generally recognised as the high point of Naipaul's art, *A House for Mr. Biswas*: two British views, one highly appreciative, one less so, and two measured West Indian ones:

Francis Wyndham:

> Conceived and executed within the great tradition of the humanist novel, *A House for Mr. Biswas* is as subtle

and comprehensive an analysis of the colonial situation
as anything in imaginative literature. It has been widely
admired and—more important—understood. When it
came out, Naipaul was still under 30.[18]

A. C. Derrick:

In *A House for Mr. Biswas* Naipaul intensifies and
carries further the method of inflation evident in *The
Mystic Masseur*. The circumstances of Biswas's birth
set him apart from other characters in the novel, but
the particularity and importance which he has in their
eyes is preserved by Naipaul, ironically, long after
Hanuman House justifiably concludes that Biswas
'mattered little'. The action of the novel demonstrates
how finally unimportant Biswas is, how futile, and
even petty, are his gestures of non-acquiescence. He often
displays a petty cantankerousness at Hanuman House
and gives himself over to action that is a pathetic
substitute for real rebellion: the food flung out of the
window on to Owad's head; the carping names he
devises for members of the Tulsi household. It is with
some justification that Shama, Biswas's wife, describes
him as a 'barking puppy dog'. Hanuman House finally
reacts to Biswas as to the insignificant, fixing his status
without great effort. The frustrating, largely inescapable
experience of Biswas, the fact that he is swindled and
repeatedly defeated by society, suggests that the
character is really a man who is utterly unimportant
except to himself. Yet, ironically, Naipaul's mode of
portrayal seems to be taking Biswas as if he were
an important, famous, public personage. The
portentousness of the full-scale, formal, biographical
treatment of Biswas thus becomes a satiric device that
mocks the ineffectiveness of the character and his
ultimate compromising of an ideal. The cold detachment
which Naipaul preserves through the sardonically
grandiose presentation of Biswas induces the reader to
set little store by what the character does achieve. It

even seems to cheapen Biswas's insight in recognising some of the limitations of his social environment, his courage in wanting to rebel against it, and his resilience in trying to achieve something worthwhile to himself, even if the attempts are largely futile. Naipaul, perhaps too obviously, puts his thumb on the scale to pull down the balance against Biswas's struggle.[19]

Gordon Rohlehr:

> *A House for Mr. Biswas* is more profound than anything else Naipaul has written because, for the first time, he is able to feel his own history not merely as a squalid farce, but as an adventure in sensibility. . . . The book can be interpreted on several levels. There is the obvious surface level where Biswas can be seen as a second-generation Indian who, although rebelling against his own decaying Hindu world, cannot come to a meaningful compromise with the Creole world of Trinidad. This Creole world comes in only by implication and allusion. . . . Since the society offers him two equally terrible nightmares, isolation and non-identification are the only alternatives left to Biswas . . . The house, which Mr. Biswas determines to build as soon as he sees the Tulsi barracks at Green Vale, is more than a place where he can live. It is his personality symbolised, the private individuality which he must both build and maintain against the rest of the world. The development in Mr. Biswas's house parallels at all points his development as a person. . . . The book is powerfully symbolic, but it is never crudely or obtrusively so. If Biswas represents all the things I feel he does, it is because he is fully presented as a person whose every quirk and idiosyncrasy we know, in a world whose every sight, sound and smell is recorded with fidelity and precision.[20]

Kenneth Ramchand:

> While in his first three works, however, Naipaul was, on balance, a popular but ironic entertainer and gentle

satirist, his fourth, *A House for Mr. Biswas* (1961), establishes him as the author of a major twentieth-century novel on the increasingly rare scale of *Middlemarch*, *Anna Karenina* or *The Rainbow*. The three-generation span of the novel gives free play to Naipaul's favourite pattern of authorial stage-setting summary followed by abundantly rendered and partly illustrative episode; and the wide cast of secondary characters allow the author's manner of swift and vivid characterization, enriched by occasional glimpses in depth, to operate with reasonable legitimacy. There are other significant developments. Instead of a vacuous character like Ganesh, the central figure is Mohun Biswas, journalist, visualized in depth as a man aware of the void of his own future and the obscurity of his origin, desperately seeking to make a dent on the world. With the creation of such a centre of interest and involvement as Mr. Biswas, the mock-biographer of *The Mystic Masseur* is replaced by the alternately ironic and caressive tones of an omniscient narrator not always able to remain on the controlling periphery.[21]

One suspects that the world of *A House for Mr. Biswas* is one modelled upon a society from which the author has himself wished to escape, and that this attitude is the source of some of the over-emphasis in the fictional construct. But if Mr. Biswas finds his world a deterrent to ambition, as well as engulfing and repulsive, the faith in life with which his author endows him, his obstinate knowledge 'that below it all there was an excitement which was hidden but waiting to be grasped' is greater than the fictional character's impulse to escape. When Mr. Biswas acquires his house he does not so much create order as confirm its possibility. However wry the accompanying gestures, this is Naipaul's precarious achievement too.[22]

The variety of views I have quoted in this section, reverential, respectful, furious, discriminating, contemptuous, is only what we should expect about a writer so gifted and so different, and about work so intricate and rich which blends enigmatically the personal and the impersonal. It seems to me particularly appropriate at this point to allow this detached author, detached that is except for the splendid commitment of his work, to speak in his own *persona*:

> I think that one has luck in all writing. One has luck
> right at the beginning when you are just starting to
> try to write. How difficult it is then to give your work
> authority. And then, after a lot of trial and error, one
> day a kind of miracle occurs. And the lines you write
> do have authority. You somehow have learnt to shape a
> paragraph a little bit more, and it's more than just a
> piece of prose. There's that character in Chekhov's
> play, *The Seagull*: they all talk about writing and
> they're all very wise about writing there, and one of
> these idle figures in the background tells the young
> man who's trying to write: 'Have an idea. Otherwise
> you won't be able to write, and you'll be destroyed by
> your talent.' You know, one has to stumble on this
> truth oneself. To have an idea. It's very hard to explain
> this; it's very hard to teach this to someone who is
> learning to write. But I've stumbled on it. I know what
> it means. And I was lucky. With every book there has
> been this element of luck, I feel, in the actual writing.
> You begin with very vague ideas. And the act of
> writing, or devising a story or form, is such an artificial
> thing: you have to woo life into this artificial thing—
> which doesn't even exist. . . . One is in love with the concept
> of being a writer. I suppose it probably goes back to my
> childhood. I used to see my father writing—my father
> tried to write and wrote stories. But until I was quite
> old I never even tried, because no miracle was occurring.
> I had nothing to write about. And I think one still
> feels like that: before a book, one is empty.
> 'Unfurnished entrails'—that was what Shaw said about
> himself when he was writing novels in the early days.
> One has to provide a book out of one's unfurnished

entrails. One still has to do this wooing. If I say I was lucky with this book, I mean that as you get older there's so many more things to feel, so many more experiences that you can have. The promptings for a book are so manifold, and to find a kind of framework which will carry all the promptings and express them fully—that requires luck. . . . Just to settle down and convert an idea into words on a page, and to let that have authority and life—I think that too requires an awful lot of luck.[23]

Naipaul's luck is his readers' fortune.

References

Chapter 1

1. *An Area of Darkness*, 1964, p. 34.
2. *The Middle Passage*, 1962, p. 47.
3. *ibid.* p. 41.
4. *ibid.*
5. *ibid.* p. 82.
6. *The Listener*, Thursday 25 Nov. 1971, Vol. 86, no. 2226.
7. *A Manifold Voice*, London (Chatto and Windus) 1970, pp. 62–3
8. *The Middle Passage*, p. 40.
9. *ibid.* p. 57.
10. *ibid.* p. 68.
11. *The Mystic Masseur*, 1957, pp. 25–6.
12. *The Suffrage of Elvira*, 1958, p. 74.
13. *A Manifold Voice*, p. 70.
14. *The Listener*, Thursday 7 Oct. 1971, Vol. 86, no. 2219.

Chapter 2

1. F. R. Leavis, *The Common Pursuit*, London (Chatto and Windus), 1952, p. 213.
2. *The Middle Passage*, Foreword.
3. *ibid.* p. 58.
4. *ibid.* p. 80.
5. *ibid.* p. 78.
6. *ibid.* pp. 66–7.
7. *ibid.* p. 66.
8. *ibid.* p. 47.
9. *ibid.*
10. *ibid.* p. 41.
11. *ibid.*

12. *ibid.* p. 62.
13. *ibid.* pp. 84–5.
14. *An Area of Darkness*, 1964, p. 15.
15. *ibid.* p. 79.
16. *The Loss of El Dorado*, 1969, Prologue, p. 10.

Chapter 3

1. F. R. Leavis, *The Great Tradition*, London (Chatto and Windus), 1948, p. 29.
2. *A House for Mr. Biswas*, 1961, p. 213.
3. *ibid.* pp. 260–1.
4. *ibid.* p. 267.
5. *ibid.* p. 15.
6. *ibid.* p. 266.
7. *ibid.* p. 285.
8. Henry James, *The Art of the Novel*, New York (Charles Scribner's Sons), 1934, p. 231.
9. *Mr. Stone and the Knights Companion*, 1963, p. 9.
10. *A Flag on the Island*, 1967, p. 9.
11. *ibid.* pp. 74–5.
12. *ibid.* p. 124.
13. *ibid.* p. 144.
14. *ibid.* p. 151.
15. *ibid.* pp. 156–7.
16. *ibid.* p. 168.

Chapter 4

1. *The Mimic Men*, 1967, p. 61.
2. *ibid.* p. 231.
3. *ibid.* pp. 263–4.
4. *ibid.* p. 219.
5. *The Listener,* Thursday 25 Nov. 1971, Vol. 86, No. 2226.
6. Henry James, *The Art of the Novel*, New York (Charles Scribner's Sons), 1934.

7. *In A Free State*, 1971, p. 25.
8. *ibid.* p. 37.
9. *ibid.* p. 61.
10. *ibid.* p. 73.
11. *ibid.* pp. 105–6.
12. *ibid.* p. 255.

Chapter 5

1. *The Listener,* Thursday 7th Oct. 1971, Vol. 86, no. 2219.
2. *The London Magazine,* Sept. 1959, Vol. 6, No. 9, pp. 80–1.
3. *The Listener,* Thursday, 7th Oct. 1971, Vol. 86, No. 2219.
4. *An Area of Darkness,* p. 37.
5. George Lamming, *The Pleasures of Exile,* London (Michael Joseph), 1960, p. 225.
6. 'The Ironic Approach: The Novels of V. S. Naipaul', in *The Islands in Between* (ed. Louis James), O.U.P., 1968, p. 122.
7. *ibid.* p. 139.
8. *ibid.* pp. 130–1.
9. 'The Search for Identity in the Caribbean', *Planet*, No. 4, 1961, pp. 57–8.
10. 'Naipaul's Technique as a Novelist', *J.C.L.,** July 1969, No. 7, pp. 32–3.
11. *The West Indian Novel and its Background,* London (Faber and Faber), 1970.
12. 'The Myth of El Dorado in the Caribbean Novel', *J.C.L.,* June 1971, Vol. VI, No. 1, p. 113.
13. *ibid.* pp. 114–16.
14. Prema Nandakumar, *The Glory and the Good,* Asia Publishing House, London 1966, p. 267.
15. 'Somewhere Something has Snapped', *The Literary Criterion,* Summer 1965, pp. 85–96.
16. 'Criticism from India', *J.C.L.,* July 1967, No. 3, p. 123.
17. 'Meeting Extremes', *J.C.L.,* September 1965, No. 1, pp. 171–2.
18. *The Listener,* Thursday 7th Oct. 1971, Vol. 86, No. 2219.
19. 'Naipaul's technique as a Novelist', *J.C.L.,* July 1969, No. 7, pp. 38–9.

20. 'The Ironic Approach', *The Islands in Between*, pp. 132–8.
21. *The West Indian Novel and its Background*, pp. 7–8.
22. *ibid*, p. 204.
23. *The Listener*, Thursday 25th Nov. 1971, Vol. 86, No. 2226.

* Note: here and in following references:
J.C.L. Journal of Commonwealth Literature.

Bibliography

1   Naipaul

The Mystic Masseur, London (André Deutsch) 1957, Russell Edition.
The Suffrage of Elvira, London (André Deutsch) 1958, Russell Edition.
Miguel Street, London (André Deutsch) 1959, Russell Edition.
A House for Mr. Biswas, London (André Deutsch) 1961, Russell Edition.
The Middle Passage, London (André Deutsch) 1962.
Mr. Stone and the Knights Companion, London (André Deutsch) 1963.
An Area of Darkness, London (André Deutsch) 1964.
The Mimic Men, London (André Deutsch) 1967.
A Flag on the Island, London 1969, Penguin.
The Loss of El Dorado, London (André Deutsch) 1969.
In a Free State, London (André Deutsch) 1971.

2   Others

COULTHARD, G. R., 'The Search for Identity in theCaribbean', *Planet,* No. 4, 1961, pp. 48ff.
DAVIES, M. BRYN, 'Criticism from India', *J.C.L.,* July 1967, no. 3, pp. 123f.
DERRICK, A. C. 'Naipaul's Technique as a Novelist', *J.C.L.,* July 1969, no. 7, pp. 32ff.
LAMMING, GEORGE, *The Pleasures of Exile,* London (Michael Joseph), 1960.
Listener, The, Thursday 25th Nov. 1971, Vol. 86, no. 2226.
MAES-JELINEK, HENA, 'The Myth of El Dorado in the Caribbean Novel', *J.C.L.* June 1971, Vol. VI, no. 1, pp. 113ff.

NANDAKUMAR, PREMA, *The Glory and the Good*, London (Asia Publishing House) 1966.

NARASIMHAIAH, C. D., 'Somewhere Something has Snapped', *The Literary Criterion*, Summer 1965, pp. 83ff.

RAMCHAND, KENNETH, *The West Indian Novel and its Background*, London (Faber and Faber) 1970.

ROHLEHR, GORDON, 'The Ironic Approach', *The Islands in Between*, (ed. Louis James), O.U.P. 1968, pp. 121ff.

WALSH, WILLIAM, 'Meeting Extremes', *J.C.L.* September 1965, no. 1, pp. 169ff.

——— *A Manifold Voice*, London (Chatto and Windus) 1970.

WYNDHAM, FRANCIS, *The London Magazine*, Sept. 1959, Vol. 6, no. 9. pp. 78ff.

——— *The Listener*, Thursday 7th Oct. 1971, Vol. 86, No. 2219.